2

Je Corseau Complete

The Anthology

Copyright 2024

Tribute

I sing ye verse of poets olde
Their songs neer afore told
With hearts then first open
In words painful spoken
To death and love centuries olde
By Chaucer and Godfrey and all
Their words so gently fall
Neer forgotten nor forgave
But trailed lonely and despaired
As if only they who cared
Wrote poems as these with broken heart
For all to hear and see love depart
With tears to blind the crying eyes
Listened all with words afore they died.
To battles of death they bragged about
Praising the clashes of a knight's bout
The death of enemies before unknown
With angers sown into valor alone
These poems cast out anonymous
To peoples taught it's animus
Who listen to the poet's lyre
Played gently with the poet's verse
To make them march to songs of war
In lands not known afore
To the Blakes, Donnes and olde Dunbar,
Poets of centuries, ages past, who
Gave somber words all wisdom cast.

To these and more these poems I write
Thrown into today's bright light
Unshielded by the body exposed
No different than written by those
Who wrote first their rhyming prose.

Introduction

It took centuries for the basic styles of poetry to morph from meter and rhyme written by Lords and Knights and Earls sitting about their castles to become prose in the mid-1800s. It is generally credited to Walt Whitman who imprinted upon his poetry new subject matters, primarily describing every individual and trade in America virtually by name to change the olde subjects into Patriotism, industriousness, America, sexuality, and every adventure one could imagine, and more. But reading Tennyson's "Ulysses" one can see how Whitman may have discovered rhyme didn't matter, but meter made the poem sing.

No more helpless damsels, gods prevailing, Christian themes or conquering battles in faraway lands. Now it was the big city, strangers in the night, the Civil War, The Mexican War, setting out to sea, The death of Lincoln, and all things here in America. And it was a celebration of himself, his empathy, more than anything. It is difficult to read the final draft of Leaves of Grass and not realize how far he had separated us from the ancient poets of olde. His influence led us to the Modernists and to the beatniks of the 20th Century. And here we are in the 21st Century still improving, still changing styles; and although meter and rhyme are somewhat out of place, they still have their place, albeit in simpler forms than prose has to offer.

JC   1/1/2024

Tribute 5

Introduction 7

List of Titles   8

The Wind howls   15

The Bridge   16

The mountain 17

Speaking to the moon 18

Tucking in the dead   19

Inspiration   20

Geese at the door   21

12-year-old gigolo   22

The Barn owl 23

This ship   24

We walk a line   25

Corn for grits 26

Before I die   27

She sat across the table   29

Memories of yours and mine   30

Road to Taos   31

Shadows   32

Vietnam   33

Let it be 34

You see me late at night   35

A poem well written   36

Been in the hole too long   37

Rattler   38

To be a six year old   39

Devin Huxley   40

Ojibwe dancers 41

He's my horse   42

Too beautiful to be alone 43

Baxter street Leroy 44

Story of dead bill   45

Bumble bee 46

A poem David Mason style 47

Pages Bent to mark each line 48

Emancipation 49

Ungrateful exit 50

This vast room 51

Like a naked child 52

Riding up Powell street 53

He rampages 54

Room of chairs 55

Survivors 56

Blue moon 57

To change a fool 58

Sylvia   59

The letters she sends   60

Santa Cruz afternoon 61

Vikings 62

I've written sonnets to the sun   63

I've begged the moon   64

The train   65

Can't forget Savannah   66

In the twilight   67

The impossible crow   68

Perhaps I am mad again   69

The lion   70

I am not of this age   71

Bending tree 72

Stragglers   73

Eloise 74

Circular   75

The love we made   76

The bricks of hell   77

The story of Henry Lee   78

In my rags   80

Piano Player 81

Rainbows in the night   82

Statues of stone 83

Look up at me   84

My French verses 85

If I were mute   86

Tangled verses   87

To the poet who cried for Sylvia   89

Journey from Africa   89

Ode to a burro   91

Sometimes there are dreams 93

Who paints the skies   93

The canvas 94

To those lovers 95

Paint a picture Baby Jane 96

Tribute to Haiti 97

Subway funny dream 100

Denmark 102

Somewhere a lark 103

I see people 104

Heather hay 105

She wanders alone 106

From this window 107

Humankind 108

There was a time 109

Alligators 110

Spirits in the night 111

My Sidhartha 112

Colors 113

Concert 114

Travels with Izzy 115

My Maine coon 116

As I Passed by 117

Elves 119

Lyrics 120

Ode to Mr. Poe 121

The pit 122

A Keg O' beer 123

It is late 124

Dawn 125

Kiss the sun 126

Dreams   127

Lovers   128

Empty soul   129

Watching it end   130

The stream   131

We are never alone   132

Greeting the rain   133

Drums   134

Asphalt   135

Did you hear Death has died?   136

The towne crier   138

Ode to Masefield   139

The devil's coach   140

She sips her cherry brew   141

Yellow giant bird   143

The death of Simeon Adele   148

Greenland   149

Homeless promenade   154

Frenchman in the garden   157

Questions for a traveler   158

The old tree   160

The old captain   162

Letters to Lorraine   165

(The Letters) 165

Winter 1838   166

Spring 1839   167

Summer 1839   168

Fall   1839   170

Andrew   171

Maggie   172

The Ojibwe 174

The Wolf 175

(The journey) 176

Leaving for Le Sault   176

The fur trader   177

Les Sault   180

The Juno   181

The last day   183

Going home   186

The dream   187

The Ojibwe camp   189

Food and play   191

The river trail   192

The cabin   194

Pictures of my family   196

Morning   197

Andrews family   198

(In my nights)   199

Reviews   202

Intro to Resurrecting the Muse   204

Je Corseau Complete

ANTHOLOGY

The Wind Howls

The wind howls like an injured animal at night
      Yesterday as she blew silently across the plains
She seemed to whisper secrets in my ear
      Like the ghost of a goddess passing by
Seeking company and a place to rest
      Now she wants nothing to do with me
As she howls madly through the darkened sky
      Her gentle touch is gone as if to say good bye
Though her journey never ends
      Tis sad I can't go with her so I blow her a kiss
But I know she will return another day
      To whisper again her secrets in my ear

The Bridge

The bridge shakes as the storm rages
> The clouds are thick and dark

the rains fall heavy upon it
> The river rushes with the strength

Of ocean waves pounding the pylons
> Logs rushing down the river

are an army of battering rams
> Assailing the very foundation

Each log a soldier
> I cannot tell what holds the bridge together

Nor why it is not swept away
> But somehow it stays together

The rain ceases to pelt
> the stream begins to slow

Until at last the logs stop
> As if patience has parted the clouds

As if time has allowed the sun to shine again
> And this bridge still stands

battered and rusted and stronger

The Mountain

Each day I climb higher

    Every morning I am closer to the sun

Each night is colder than before

    The fire is a good friend

At night an animal stalks

    I hear it breaking twigs

As I walk through the trees

    But it will not let me see it

It hides in the maze of the forest

    Maybe when there are no more trees

And there's no place to hide

    Then I will know what stalks me

But that is many days ahead

    And I have so much farther to go

Speaking To The Moon

Sometimes when I am speaking to the moon
     And our talk ends as morn comes too soon
I tell the sun "Please don't interrupt
     We are having a private conversation
It's not for you to interrupt so abrupt
     About our secretly held relations
To the beauty of the darkness and the night
     And you, Mr. Sun,
with your overpowering light
     Come between us in such a rude manner
Like a screaming 'patriot' with his banner
     Imprinted with the name of what's-his-name
Wanting to change it all back to the same
     Sad conditions we suffered before
And I have to ask "what do they have in store."
     Meanwhile the moon and I are having an affair
With the stars without any of those cares
     Or about those mottos and daytime chores
That just light up the political whores
That cause us to close our eyes to the moon
And forget to embrace the stars too soon
Who cradle us through the evening hours
Like a lover bringing home a bouquet of flowers

Tucking in the Dead

One night past as I wandered by the cemetery at dusk
I wondered how the dead must sleep
Had they blankets for the night to keep them warm
Should I stroll by each mound and see?
And tuck them in one by one
To be sure their toes stay warm
And fluff their pillows nice and neat
Perhaps recite a bedtime story for them all
In hopes to hear them snuggling loud below..
When passing by an old friend who stopped amused
To tell me how all below are dead and gone
Not to be found there anymore
For they are now in heaven and hell
Where comforts hand can reach them no more
Nor give them the solace of our earthen warmth
So I turned and saluted them all on their journeys
Bid them farewell and offered my hand
Whether they be stepping down or stepping up
I have to feel pity it is too late to offer them
What I can no longer give.

Inspiration

Inspiration is everywhere.

It can be a lanky woman in a red dress

I found it there sometime without the dress

Or the moon hiding behind a black cloud

A basketball child who sinks a basket

It can be waves crashing against cliffs

Or a leaf on the ground rolling over with the wind

Everyone finds it in a red sunset upon the sea

Or the way a flower grows and blooms

Or the way the moon looks down and smiles

It's everywhere you look

It's everything you feel

It's a thought it's an idea it's heartbreak

It is there with sorrow

It is there with joy

Geese at the Doorway

The night has left a soft cover of snow for the morning.
     The geese wander to the opened door of my den.
They think as usual they are allowed to visit and come in
     Like any other day, but I have to say not now
Their feet are wet with snow and mud
     So I close the door with a gentle thud
But they so stubborn lay down outside
     Until better weather is on their side
(I only suppose that is how they think)
     Who knows what is on their minds?
They know I like them in and set out water to drink
     So they wait for the door until they find
A way to get by its invisible wall
     And hear my beckoning call
Sweet birds they, so mis-aligned....
     No one seems to see their gentler side
But I always do
     Maybe you should see them untie my boots
When home from working I sit down to rest
     And they flock around to welcome me back
And the best I can do is stroke a feather or two.

Twelve-Year-Old Gigolo

Robbie was a gigolo
> Tall for his age

Maybe too smart, too
> Standing on the corner

The fagolos always gave him the eye
> The town was too small not to notice

His parents drunk and out of control
> At twelve he controlled his own world

The sheriff never cared it seemed
> Sometimes he would get a ride and be gone for a day.

One day he never returned.

The Barn Owl

The barn owl sings his hoot hoot song

"Come out come out wherever you are."

But the mice aren't listening

They'll have nothing of that

So all the barn owl can do

Is sing his hoot hoot song

This Ship

This ship flounders with uneven tides
      Some waves rock it like a baby's cradle
Other waves threaten to sweep it away
      Breaking violently over the decks
That is the daily rhythm of its voyage
      Sometimes it is the wind that forces
 the lowering of the sails
      Which leaves this ship floundering?
With no means of steerage
      It is then the victim of an angry sea
With only providence to save the day

We walk a line

Every day we walk a line

      Between what we want and what we need

And again what we must do to survive

      Every day we balance ourself

Least we miss a step

      And fall from this precarious journey.

Corn for grits

Corn for grits
>
> Goats for milk

Beets for sugar
>
> Hens for eggs

Pigs for bacon

...and pheasants in the field.
>
> Ain't no starving on the farm

Before I Died

Before I died I asked the sky

    "Is there a heaven up there and do the dead

have private rooms

Or do they all bunk together like triplets in the womb?"

    The sky looked down and said "You'll have to come up and see."

"Not today, Sky. Guess I'll find out when I get there."

That night, when the sky was asleep, I had a dream.

    In the dream

I floated up behind a napping cloud

    where darkness hid me.

Some were playing cards

    And others it was charades.

Shuffleboard seemed a favorite.

    And many sat in rockers knitting sweaters and such.

This all seemed quite logical given their ages.

    They all seemed very happy with their lot.

Most seemed to have perished from too many years

    While others it was obvious they had been shot.

But over-all I judged their end to be caused

    By boredom and a lack of company.

The next day when the sky woke up

    I told it about my dream

I asked if this could possibly be the truth.

    The sky nodded and said,

"Yes. This is what awaits you.

    "You've wandered onto the fact of it all,

but you should not tell anyone what you've seen."
I've thought a bit about it now and I'm not sure
If death is all it's cracked up to be.

She sat across the table

She sat across the table with shimmering breasts..
That shook with every word she uttered
And though she spoke incessantly I couldn't hear a word
These two things combined I wished she'd give a rest
How is a man supposed to concentrate on the menu
With such distractions in the summer heat
And the background noise of traffic on the avenue

Shimmering breasts yak yak yak and sirens in the street
How was I to know if I was horny or hungry?
Having had enough of this confusion I stood up and said
"Order whatever you like, I'm going to wash my hands."
I hated to leave her that way and I hope she understands
I also hope she brings her credit card just in case
She runs into another man who's lost his ability to think.

Memories of Yours and Mine

The memories of mine and yours are the .same

    With tenderness, reverie, laughter, adventure

Untouched by age or new times, held together.

    By visions, dreams, felt physically in dreams such as these.

Where we never part except by death,

     yes of course by death,

    But not by life. Not in life, not today or now, because it does not part us.

It may only separate us for a spell, but that is not the same as parted.

    These memories are the same but not the same,

    Just harnessed in different minds in different ways.

Road to Taos

I had taken this same old van to Mexico

But we stayed too briefly

My friends had business back in Los Angeles

Now I have two different passengers

Janet is portly and a beautiful friend

James is gay and along for the ride and hates Janet

It's hard to drive on a quarreling bus

The ride is long but seems forever

I have to deal with James's attacks on Janet

Janet wants to turn back but it's too late

I wanted to leave James on the side of the road

But we were too close to Taos now

In Sante Fe I called my friend Justice

He met us at the Greyhound station

Where I think he saw the problem

We never made it to the reservation

Janet seemed to fall in love with Justice right away

I left her there because that is what she wanted

That evening as I drove back toward Los Angeles

I had to listen to James' lingering hate for Janet

I believe it was in Barstow at a gas station

James went inside to use the bathroom

I didn't feel guilty as I drove away

I saw him in my rearview mirror waving frantically

I had gained a lesson

I saw love and hate divide the day

I saw one win and the other lose

And I saw Justice for the last time

Shadows

I have asked the sun to rise and cast shadows

    I have asked the shadows to move with the sun

They have both complied obediently

    There are times when I follow the shadows

A shadow always follows me

    I do not talk to the shadows

They never talk to me

    But we are friends and we know each other

I thank the sun for the shadows

At night when the sun sleeps

    I ask the moon and the city lights to cast shadows

But without them, and there are those times,

    There are only silhouettes behind drawn blinds

And outlines against starry skies

    I thank the heavens for this

I think the shadows must miss the day

    The day is when I've seen them mingle and play

It's when they can talk to each other

    I don't know what they would say to me

Or if they are shy when they see me here

    I thank the heavens and the sun for shadows

Vietnam

A thousand years had passed it seemed

      When I saw my old friend Johnny

Did you go to the war. I remember you hiding in a church

                No. They said I had flat feet

All that hiding for nothing

What about the other guys we hung with

            Willie came back angry and crazy

            No longer like a kid

What about Dave who rode the Harley

          Heroin! All strung out   It killed him

I've seen Tom Kletch in LA He's a plumber now

His little brother is on heroin too

           Danny was excused Too gay to
serve

           The others I don't know…

      Cannon fodder I guess

Never came back

What happened to Norm

           He was smart Joined the navy

           He's a big CEO now

Good for him

           What about you, Did you go

No. Heart Murmur. I stayed home

And wrote bad poetry

Let It Be

I would have stayed with you had you allowed it
        I didn't care for the agonies or the anger
Or the times you threw a fit
                There were better times
                Do you remember
It's true that love is blind
I remember the fits of December
                The stress of too many eves
Passover Christmas New Years Birthdays
The liquor made your mother pass away
        The eves were the rites of trauma you believed
Your violence was impossible to understand
But I would have stayed if you'd allowed it
        And why Passover? You aren't even Jewish
It was just another trauma to cause a fit
                Brokenhearted love departed
It was all just yesterday
        Stranded by the wayside
                Bags of belongings on the porch
                Kicking bags of love aside
I would have stayed if you'd allowed it
        I tolerated it all and
Understood none of it. I let it be

You See Me Late At Night

You see me late at night
      Struggling with difficult words
I see you walking by in your evening dress
      The hours tick by
In the morning I wake in a cloudy daze
      And you are asleep beside me
Good, I will throw my arm around you
      I feel your stomach warm and tight
Your thighs smooth skinny and bony
      Nothing else could wake me like this
I want to slide my hand over your every part
      But coffee seems a more appropriate task
Especially when I should let you sleep
      You are lucky You have missed nothing
And I have strange words to untangle

A Poem Well Written

A poem well written
  With deep roots in the heart
Releases the imprisoned soul
  And the two are content
To live together never apart
  Not one nor the other
To give its consent
  To say how it feels
Or draw images of its depths

Been In The Hole Too Long

Been in the hole for days and days
Don't know what I did wrong
Just jumped two bandits who wanted my stuff
Couldn't just let them go
Can't let nothing go in here. Nothing
Can't let anybody think you're easy
Then the time gets hard to do
Predators Predators everywhere
Here I have a hole in the floor for a toilet
Gotta make sure you don't miss
And got a sink! Goddam got a sink!
Got a two inch mattress to sleep on
Outside the bars just a wide empty hall
With bars where the windows should be
There's yelling for entertainment
And frozen bricks of leftovers for food
From what the prisoners don't eat
At least in the hole you get your own room
Might get out of here someday. Don't know when
The guy next to me been here a year
Push ups and knee bends about all you can do
Maybe soon I'll hear the keys walking my way.
But not too long from today. I hope.
I need my sanity….and my stuff

Rattler

The boys came running in with the dog excited

Leading me to the Oaktree with the swing

A rattler coiled asleep in its shade

It seemed harmless. I thought it was dreaming

>But they had brought me here to kill it

>"Aw, Maybe he's just waiting his turn on the swing"

>They saw no humor in that. "No! Kill it! Kill it."

>The boys came running in with the dog very excited.

The oldest handed me a shovel. I said "Leave it be."

They threw rocks to shoo it away

But it only slithered closer than away

Now facing a coiled rattler I had no choice

>I waited for him to strike and with a sharp plunge

>I had cut off his head "Hold back the dog."

>"I get dibs on his head."

>"Not yet. His head can still strike."

"I want his rattle" shouted another

We waited until they had fetched a mason jar

With frightful skill they captured the head

To the boys it was an adventure. It couldn't wait

>And only I could kill the scary reptile

>For this honor I was hero for a day

>They were thrilled with their trophies

>I looked and the dog was still trembling

To Be A 6 Year Old

To be a 6-year-old busy cutting asparagus
Low to the ground is how I got the job

    Cutting spears crouched like a monkey

    Row after row in September's heat

In a field small enough for a child
All for a chance to play in the cool evening

    Then dancing and darts with a target on the barn

    To be a 6 year old and work on the farm

To be a 6 year old and mama tucks you in at night
To dream of the asparagus giant who eats 6 year olds

    In the morning a cool breeze in the window

    Crows in the field eating corn on the cob

The plowed field full of overturned rocks
A hawk flies over with a snake in its talons

    Today we throw rocks on the scow behind the mule

    It's all low to the ground work. It's how I got the job.

Devin Huxley

Now I will sing a long lost love song

To a brother-friend of my past and after

Who embraced my life with his childish joys

In games of sweet adventure and laughter

With explorations in the hallowed hills of troy

 make-believe battles fought in darkened Bronson caves.

Where the sun never dared go

Play wars that ripped away the daily trends

And left us standing friend to friend.

Now I have so say goodbye to this beautiful soul

While cancer divides us and brings an end

To this song I will never sing again

…to this man who taught me to be a child once more

When we toyed with the movie makers

Who shouted "Quiet on the set" and we laughed out loud

And we trudged those hills like sylvan lions

  And met the Orions of the night in silver shrouds

  As though we owned the trails to heaven

  Playing as if the song would never end

  Though I cannot stop hearing its sweet rhapsody

  Deep in my heart longing for that day again

There were days when he brought home the children of the street

To sleep on our floor and share our linen sheets

That incredible open-arms man who always slept alone

Has passed and left his hand upon my heart

Ojibwe Dancers

I want to speak to the hawk about soaring over my head
With a snake in its claws writhing to get free
I want him to teach me how to fly so easily
How to swoop down and snatch the snake
Elders tell me I can be the hawk
I can dance with his feathers in my hair
When the elders dance they are eagles
They are bears and they are cougars
They are coyotes and they are wolves
But no one wants to be the snake

He Is My Horse

My horse runs away and hides in the field
When he sees me drag his saddle out
He does not like the saddle. It is not a part of him
He knows this and does not want it on his back
But if he sees me walking
With no saddle following me
He will come and lower his head
Until I can shinney up on his back
Naked without the saddle
Because he knows that I am part of him.
He is my horse and I am his child.

Too Beautiful to be alone

She sits on the rocks along the creek
The water rippling by with angelic voice
Her brown skin shining like the water deep
In her head hearing the tribal songs and dance
Lilting soft and gently with steady drumbeat
With her feet hanging loosely in the flowing water
And in her heart the blood gives a sweet reply
With the early moon above watching through the clouds
The setting sun nodding quietly on her braids
The stars soon awakening playing in the sky
-these are all the children of the night-
Swirling with the galaxies as the earth turned
While below on the rocks this maiden sits alone
The waters flowing cooly over her feet and now
Sinking in naked with breasts tingling with the chill
No one to take her or visit her sadness still
Or fill her empty soul or dress her heart with love

  (Along the creek the trees all look down

  Holding out their limbs to shelter her)

Too beautiful to be alone

Baxter Street Leroy

Now's the time to bury Baxter Street Leroy
        With all the ladies cryin' boo hoo
And the boys he saddened too
        How odd them too he kept
And mothers on the casket wept
It's all done with now he's dead
Shalene said she done it
        Shot him in his bed
Caught him with another whore
        He won't do that no more
Now he rides down Baxter Street
        His coffin wrapped in a black silk sheet
So goodbye Baxter Street Leroy, listen to the ladies sob,
        A new pimp's gon' take your job.

The Story of Dead Bill

It was Bill the pescaderian advopole
Who, saddened by his own death, could not be conjoled
Who spent all his wife's inheritance on a flock of geese
Then ran home to ask her to forgive him please
But she seemed disturbed and grabbed him by the collar
And said "You fool! That was thirty dollars!"
His uncle Benny came in with an aardvark under his arm
And said, "If you weren't dead I would do you harm."
His wife said, "That's it, Bill, It's time you were embalmed."
And proceeded without asking to read his palm.
But bill continued to offer up his defense
When all the geese flew over the back fence.
"You were no good alive and now you're worse dead."
Said she, and picked up a violin and hit him over the head.
This didn't bother Bill. He was glad it wasn't the piano.
Besides, he was dead and didn't feel a thing.
He said he felt bad and would pay it all back,
Except they took him outside and buried him.
This, of course, is the end of the story
And, also, the end of dead Bill

Bumblebee

Today I came upon a giant bumblebee
Hovering about a lavender bloom
Just as busy as a bee can be
Completely ignoring me so I gave him room
I reached out for him to land on my hand
But the fact I was a friend he did not understand
And kept about his business of pollinating
And I, feeling rejected we weren't relating,
Went on about my way
Sorry he would not play with me.
Maybe he noticed I was not a bumblebee.

A Poem David Mason style

I don't recall how the old Buick still ran
But it got me across town to an audition site.
I was waiting for my chance to audition for a soap
When I heard murmured voices of the news.

Anita, already a star, was my audition partner that day.
Where was she? Impatient I called her.
She had heard the news. She was not coming.
I went back to the Buick and started driving.
It didn't matter where. I just drove aimlessly
All around Hollywood with the radio on.
The radio people knew nothing. Only he had been shot.
Then after a while I heard this: "The President is dead."

Just like that. I kept driving and in disbelief.
Finally, I parked the Buick in West Hollywood.
I left it there with steam billowing from under the hood.
I went inside Gee Gees restaurant and sat at the counter.
Some loud guy was happy about the assassination.
It didn't take long before the sheriff took him away.

       I didn't call Anita again. I just put water in the Buick
       And drove over the hill to her house.
       I told her about the audition crowd and the loud guy.
       We sat and listened some more. There were a few
       Tears. …. We never auditioned together after that.

Pages Bent To Mark Each Line

Pages bent to mark each line
      as I read each rhyme with wonder.
I'll get to them someday soon
      when there's time to read my own
on those dark and lazy afternoons
      When confusion and odes combine
to grapple with the inner reasons
      that seek answers to these rhymes.
They are driven by calculations.
      of how the past went by so fast
in all its manipulations.
      So many pages to turn.
I'll read it all someday
      before I walk away.

Emancipation

At last these bonds are unleashed

These ropes untied

Freedom at last untried

No master is pleased his slaves are released

No cell or cabin still latched shut

The wardens souls hung on Christian crosses

No guards to issue tortured losses

All retracted from a nightmare's bloodshed

Now drinking the sweet wine of freedom

While they throw their shackles down

Tearing away the bars of Edom

Ephemeral and airborne blown

These chains are now unleashed

The people at last released

No bondsman left to watch over them

No hounds to bay and track them down

Beyond these gates of hell

To where they finally in peace can dwell

"Free at last! Free at last!" cries the minister

It is the end of all things sinister

It lies ahead in the land of liberty

Sweet Jesus give us this day of charity

Ungraceful exit

This ungraceful exit has been going on for some time
The little wounds have healed over
and the bad notes have drifted away
Sometimes the person who touches your heart
 becomes someone else and takes a different path
 I will not miss this new person
because I have already cried at the loss
of the one who touched my heart

About This Vast Room

About this vast room of the living
We mourn with greater sadness
The loss of those we loved...

> Do we mourn softly in our sleep
> And, as we weep, dampen the sheets
> And pillows with tears of sorrow
> To dry in tomorrow's memories...

Memories of the joys of life now withdrawn
By these tragedies we have invented,
Brought upon ourselves, created by
Human hatred, jealousy, avarice, fear,
Prejudice, selfishness and intolerance?

> Or do we mourn that we are human'
> Unable to comprehend the gift we've been given,
> And allow the carnage to continue ad infinitum,
> With no changes made, no adjustment to our nature?

Man is but a foolish creature bound by suicide,
Self-extinction and mutual genocide;
A waste of God's favorite creation.

Like a Naked Child

Like a child running naked through the forest
Joining his friends in the arroyo's swimming pond
On those hot days jumping in with the rest
And all standing naked together drying on the shore
No one to tell them they must dress themselves
Such freedom only a child can possess
I was that child…Now I wear clothes

Riding up Powell Street

Riding up Powell Street
In a cable car full of donut eating tourists
There's a blond boy sleeping with a Canadian sailor
Motel and money he's in love
Food for sex and a place to sleep
Sailor his age at sea too long
Never to be seen again he's gone to sea
A whore from home the boy knows
She's a neighbor from the suburbs
Working the tenderloin
The sun goes down the night goes on
Can the Canadian navy support all this?
Heroin on the corner crack in the bars
Cops in paddy wagons laughing at it all
      (Ginsberg would be proud of this poem
        He would write it just like this
        With Cassidy holding his hand and his junk)
The Beats would seek to amaze
With rhetoric unheard of in their day
    But Frisco was more than hustlers and getting high
    Haight-Ashbury was not the first drug haven
    Grant street was full of hustlers and drunks on every corner
North Beach supported the Beats even before Ferlinghetti
  (Who kicked me off the steps of City Lights for reading
  Hippy poetry and playing bad guitar)
He was right; the poetry was just as bad.
I haven't been there in ages. It's probably just the same.

He Rampages

He rampages through the house
            Like a lion against his pride
The doors of the den slammed shut
            Pacing angry and proud of himself
Across the estate a threat to all
            His roar beckons loyalty without complaint
While little lions cry in the nursery alone
            The pride is broken by words misspoken
The house now an untamed jungle
            Of emotions uncontrolled unthawed
The ice in the heart breaking the glass
            The glass spilling its contents of anger
Wasted in a moment of lies and rage
            He expects us to forget this moment
To close our eyes and turn the page
            To think this insanity never happened
Yet we all saw it, We heard it, We felt it
We will not forget it

The Room of Chairs

Enter the King and Queen into the room of chairs.
Sitting upon the thrones, they count the empty chairs.
Says he, "Too many chairs;' Says she,"Too few people"
So they invited all their subjects in to have a seat.
But there were too many subjects and soon nowhere to sit.

So it was decreed that more chairs be brought in.
And the royal chairmaker was called in to make more.
Soon there were chairs aplenty; but, too many chairs.

Says she, "O dear, where can we get more subjects?'
Says he, "We will conquer the neighbors and use his'"
"Brilliant!" Said the Queen. And so they had a war and won,
And they brought in all these new subjects.
This worked well, until they soon ran out of chairs again.

The royal chairmaker was then summoned and told
"You must make new chairs with subjects already yon them"
Says the chairmaker, "But I can only make empty chairs"
'Blasphemy!' cried the king. 'do it or die.'
"Off with his head," cried the Queen. "Off to your shop!"
He retreated to his shop and then miraculously disappeared.
and was never seen again..

Survivors

I have seen enough of this world
To be disgusted by what I've seen
So I turn to look another way
Perhaps to find a better scenery
But it is the same old drudgery
About wars, death, starvation, and sacrifices
A planet itself melting under human weight
Humans with nowhere to hide
From what they have created
Sweltering in a search for shade
Dying from their own created Frankenstein
Glaciers plunging into a soon risen sea
As global warming creates a new ice age
Happening before our fated eyes.
Neanderthals, my ancestors, overcame it;
Cave people, hunters, artists, travelers
Far, far across Atlantic Ice, pursued by death,
Inventers of fire, heaters of seal oil, fishermen,
Tailors of Mammoth skin suits; survivors.
Populating tribes of northern America, Canada.

Blue Moons

Looking up into the dark sky
I see the blue moon rising in the east.
        Its companion moon now gone, disappeared.
Two moons in the month of August.
Mister and Missus, they are, I suppose,
        As if the stars are their children
        Scattered across the universe.
Just like the children of the earth people,
Lost among the masses of other children,
        The planets, also shine like distant relatives,
        Aunts and uncles, untouching, detached, solitary,
All spinning in orbits through the galaxies,
        Their own moons wed, magnetically to them.
        It is a wonder to behold and a memory etched
Deeply in the brain, like a tale often told.
A recurring dream, this vision in the dark sky.

To Change a Fool

It is impossible to change a fool,

Though the fool may think he is a sage.

Then, of course, he is his own tool;

An implement of ignorance at any age,

Unless the fool turns and says,

"Only a fool would attempt to change a fool."

Sylvia

I cannot make sense of the nonsense.
Wasted on a page of inert rhymes.
Sometimes reading a certain genius poet
With verses tossed in a salad of adverbs

I cannot decipher their illogical meanings
But I can read an underlying psychosis
And understand how her incarcerated poems
Lead closer and closer to her suicidal days

It was a short life for a genius poet
And her 400 or so poems of personal pain
From which I found no inspiration to write
Lest one believes this obituary ode to be inspired

The Letters She Sends

The letters she sends come every day

Each one I open has her love inside

With every new envelope our love grows

When I answer, there is so much to say

With love returned so difficult to hide

      Daily this conversation of the heart flows

Yesterday I found a pressed rose enclosed

And sent back a tear on a stained page

So she would know how deeply it made me feel

This is the essence of love's highs and lows

These tokens of our daily appendage

Enough to make a strong man his faults reveal

      Tomorrow there will be another letter

And I know what it will say to me

And I will answer and she will know

That what she has sent has made us better

As each day this faraway dance will be

Our distant romance that grows and grow

Santa Cruz Afternoon

A giant oak tree shades the coast highway
Below the waves roll in one by one
Offshore a trawler glides across the ocean
Dwarfed by the oak, it sails north past the sun's glare
Leaving a long disappearing white wake
Soon the trawler has sailed out of sight
And once again the sea is calm
The oak still stands spreading its leafy limbs
Over its own shadow on the road
The waves splash against the cliffs and rocks below
The rocks are covered with foam as the tide recedes
with her body board descends the cliffs
Walking a path through the ice plants to the water
I sit in comfort in my coach and watch
I may also be an oak, but I cast no shadow

Vikings (Not a true story)

Everyone in Finland rides white horses
Because it's illegal to dye them green
And they all keep ancient Vikings in their cellars
      (Some of them are five hundred years old)
With grey beards the length of cypress trees
But they are not allowed to ride the horses
Lest they use the privilege to pirate the Finns
Or fall seasick to the ground unsaddled
      (Such an embarrassment that would be)
And just another reason to keep them in the cellar
Once there was an outbreak of old Vikings
When many escaped from their prison cellars
      But they were all soon captured by the Finns
Who banded together to grab the loose Vikings
And tied them all together by their grey beards
And one by one returned them to their cellars
And that is where they are all kept to this day
Which is why you don't see Vikings anymore

I've written sonnets to the Sun

I've written sonnets to the sun,
Love letters to a shimmering breeze,
Erotic poetry to the passing wind and
Obituaries to the darkened soil.
These words have sought atonement
For the sins of a transgressive life
Which I have pressed upon an uneven past.
I've granted entrance upon my soul
To the crimes I left behind
Though they are gone and left in a limbo
By the wayside of this journey.
They are like the petals of flowers left as clues
Leaving only their dour scents still wafting
In the mysterious air of yesteryear.
Now like a sunflower in a rose garden
It all stands out for all to see....
No camouflage to hide the barren truth.

I've Begged The Moon

I've begged the moon
to join me in the light of day.
But she insists she loves me only
in the dark of night.

The Train

Walking down the aisle the train rattles

Doors to the suites are closed

Wonder what goes on with in each chamber

Do they Chat and drink tea oblivious to the ride?

Are children romping disturbing cramped parents

Or are lovers throwing pillows off the berths

To make room for sex inside a syncopating bedroom?

Between the cars it's fresh air and farmland spinning by

The rails clack away and the ties below pass in a blur

In the dining car the plates and glasses shimmy

Wiggling as though alive, nothing is still or calm

Outside a city approaches and buildings loom large

Entering the railyard lines of empty boxcars

Hobos sitting in the slid back open doorways

With railroad dicks chasing them off with clubs

The train insulates the passengers from all of this

As it slowly pulls into the station where people wait

To board and depart to come and go

Like life the train is a microcosm of the world

Each to his own, some getting on, some getting off

But not one rides the train forever

Can't Forget You Savannah

I can't forget you Savannah
We lived such a leisurely life
In old brick mansions that survived
The cannons of the Negro Wars

Where so many died for the freedoms
We so naively thought all possessed
Forgetting the ones called slaves
When life was a romp of leisure
At the expense of those chained who suffered

We saw them every day in our fields of cotton and corn
And here in Savannah in our homes and stores
I can't forget you Savannah
Or wishing for that time to wash away.
Today a rebuilt Savannah begs to be modern
Where each and all are the same

Where blacks and whites are neighbors
Where the black cook, the plumber, the painter
And the black cop earn a decent wage.

I can't forget you Savannah
I'm still allowed to have that memory
Where all has changed for now the better…
Where there are no chains or whips
And no tree limbs sagging with strange fruit

And In The Twilight

And in the twilight, the moons scattered glow

Casts shadows upon the sleeping stone giants

Erected to honor the past deeds of the sleeping dead

Lost at the command of those same giants,

Years ago, in battles lost and sadly won,

Upon the fields called glory and brave

Where the blood of yesteryear bleeds red today

Wooden crosses and stars strewn as far as can be seen

Litter the grounds where trees once stood

In a maze unimagined in today's youthful eyes

Whose gaze cannot comprehend what this means

Gone are the clashes of swords and bayonets

The roar of the cannon and the bursts of rifleshot

Gone the screams of calvary and the snorts of fallen horses

The dying shouts of stricken soldiers, young men

Called to a war no one can understand;

Now all buried here, unknown except to the few,

Guarded over by stone giants who ordered them to die.

The Impossible Crow

Though the wind is screaming by,

The crow clutches the crown of a bending pine.

Though invisible , I hear the wind speak.

Though unseen, it scatters all objects around

Like toys in a child's room-

Littered and in disarray-

the wind has made it's mad appointment.

It whooshes by as the trees bow to its strength.

The clap and roar of thunder

Applauds its own performance.

The crack of lightning brightens the night sky.

The crow caws from the top of the pine.

The heavens do not disturb him.

He is serene in his royal perch.

Tomorrow we will put the world back together.

The crow will look down and make his caw-caw,

His tree now standing straight again.

Perhaps I Am Mad Again

Perhaps I am mad again
A lunatic to be carried away
To a cell with no window to cast light
On the darkness that the mind creates
When sanity loses its war with depression
And logic is a rose lost in the night

     Perhaps this madness if just temporary

     And there are drugs to make it subside

     And there are doctors who know the cure

     I have not met one yet but I'm willing to wait

Meanwhile I wish they'd turn on the light
Or at least paint a window on the wall

     The nurses bring me pills at night

     To stop my screaming I suppose.

     It must keep them awake at their posts

     But I enjoy its loud release

     And mostly it puts me to sleep

But please paint a window on the wall
I want to look out and see the sun
And ask the doctor what I have done
To be put away in a concrete cell.
Maybe he knows if I'll ever be well

     Or if the nurses are poisoning me

     But at least paint a window on the wall

The Lion

The willow bends to carry the snow.
It's an early December sight to see.
The dogwoods foretold this day:
Always sensing the coming winter;
It's blossoms now gone and buried.
The lion in the bush makes a bed of brush.
She minds us not and we let her sleep'
I will add some hay when she is off.

    The snow is not enough to slide off the roof,

     But I will do well to clear off the walkway.

    December brings the clearest skies;

    It lets in the brightest sunlight.

    The clouds hide away when nighttime falls.

Angela says, "The lion is good. She keeps the coyotes away."
She is right. The nights are quieter now.
but we still hear them howling farther away,
back and forth
from one side of the mountain to the other.

    Tonight, I'll bring in more firewood

    And maybe toss some meat to the lion. She likes that.

    Angela says, "Keep that up and she'll never go away."

    That's probably why I feed her.

    Last winter she hauled home a small doe.

    No one had to feed her then.

I am not of this age

I am not a poet for this age.
I must follow like a virgin at the alter.
My bridegroom, the sage of history.
His grey-blue Rimbaud eyes
Peer through my naked thoughts.

Too late to touch the ghosts of death
Who beckon past the day of the dead
Walking past the horizon in multitudes,
Each rising, unseen, invisible,
All imbibing the whores of absinthe and hashish,
Hallucinations and phantasmagoria.

I've slept in the hollowed base of a palm tree
In the midst of a stirring metropolis,
Its neon stars lulling me to dreams
As the mists of carbon air shower my sleep.
I am a widow to the poet sage I love.
I am alive by his lost existence still.

Bending Tree

I sit on a cliff above the sea,
by an old tree bending in the wind,
While storms brew on the horizon
    (Their drumbeats silenced by distance).
I listen to the shrieks of the gulls above
And think about the nature of nature.
Waves splash the air over the docks below
Where the little boats sway in crazy rhythms.
    At night the coyotes sing an eerie chorus
    Above the peaks of the sandy dunes.
While this ocean keeps me grounded
And prevents me from going adrift.
    This nature is the nature of nature.
    It binds me to the earth as if by chains
    While my mind seeks to wander away
    Into that distant enchanting storm
    As if it's thunder and clouds beckon
    For me to come and join in its folly.

Stragglers

They are around almost every day,
Meeting in the café where they aren't allowed,
Wearing their dirty mildewed clothes,
The stench barely covering the smell of piss,
And talk about each other (who stole what, etc)
Their bags and boxes stacked by each table.
Asked to leave, they heed nothing at all.
Who cares if they stay some more?
Then they begin their arguments
As though it just occurred as something to do.
Told again to get out they heed nothing.
This all happens when they have nothing to do.
Slowly everything calms down, and one by one,
They begin to straggle out back to the street.
The waitress with the big tits takes my order.
"Bring me a draught" I watch her big ass wiggle away.
The stragglers will be back tomorrow, as will I.
The big titted waitress will bring me another beer.
I'll mostly be here for the show.

Elouise

It is the part about being apart
that tears at this ragged heart.
The time passes slowly each day
While my mind seems to wander away
to the time before I knew you
and about your wish to die so soon.

Had I seen the signs in your eyes
I would have stayed closer by your side.
But you never told me any lies
And I never asked you for the truth.
If you had, I would have stayed
And listened more closely to your words.

Now I remember the tears in your caress
Which I thought were my own in distress.
Somehow, I believe you can still hear me
As I shout these verses into nowhere.

Circular

The planets and

the orbits in the skies.

Even the paths we take.

Everything is circular

This is not a time to look away from that

Or to think there's a straight line from here to there.

Watch the moon circle the earth

And the earth the sun

And the sun the cosmos.

Watch the child spin around with glee

     And try to be that child.

     When you have done a good thing

     See how it returns to you.

     These struggles never end.

     There is a war over there

     and the armies go round and round

     with no one standing down.

          Whatever force propels us also kills us.

          It's better to be in the circle

          And start at the beginning of time.

The Love We Made

In my earliest years I'd never had such a love;
French, strong, a certain sophistication, strong,
Intelligent, sexual (what else to ask?).
Deep ebony skinned, Ethiopian, tall, tender in love,
Though demanding too strongly my obedience, loyalty.
Stay here, lie this way, be at my side when I need you,
Do not stray, hold me all night, caress me this way....

     Finally, the leash was too tight, too short.

     My dreams took we elsewhere to wander,

Places never seen, to places I'd never been, to be held
In the arms of others. And to others who take you in
As their own or to love you just as well
If not in the same way but with as much love, sexuality,
and sophistication: the difference between leader and lover.
The freedom to make choices, to return affection in kind;
To seek other playmates and lovers, but to remain loyal.
To explore, grow, expand into new meanings; to change
Into an adult. Years ago, I wrote, "I've had many lovers
and I've Forgotten all their names." Not true, I've had very
few lovers and I remember their names and the love we
made.

The Bricks of Hell

There is a joy to this insanity that takes my hand
And leads me as a child across the molten bricks
Of the road through hell to meet Satan himself,
Who sits upon Hades throne, naked, unscathed
By the inferno about him, proud,
The very creator of this fiery kingdom he rules.

Yet I find him smiling upon me in the most
Welcoming of fashions; his arms reaching out
And flailing wildly but not touching me.
I am told, should we touch, I would suddenly
Burst into flame and ashes.

I ask why I have been brought here before him.
"Could it be my vile life of sins on earth?"
"No," he says. (At this he laughed to himself).
"You are here that I may meet you first hand
and congratulate you upon your sins."
"You may leave this dream now and return to your bed."
     I awaken to the dark clothes of my burial
     Strewn about my room. Tears of sorrow
     From my mother's eyes still dampen them.

The story of Henry Lee
(A traveler from Tennessee)

The morning mist song of Henry Lee rides
the clack-clack tracks
of the Pennsylvania Road.

The Rock Island line beats a poundin' rhyme
down the nickel plate tracks
of the Burlington Road.

Take the Jersey City Road of quick thump-thumps
from Jersey City 'round
to Hoboken town.

"Imma slides back the door of ma freight car bed
and the sun's good morn'
wakes ma sleepy head.

Imma roll down the tracks and on ma way
from Amarillo, denver and Albuquerque.

Roll on freight train to the east again
'cuz its cottonpickin' time
in Crawford, Tennessee.

Ma railroad boogey-woogey beats an iron beat
of quick staccato rhythm
in September's heat.

There's a yellow old sun and the passin' blue waters
where ma chocolate brown woman
in the Windy City waits.

I's got liver and onion for ma jet black mary
and little miss easy walk
ma jelly red baby.

I's got raw eggs and sausage for ma chocolate cake
and peanut butter syrup
for ma little bronze thrill.

Ma butterscotch baby feeds me hot rice biscuits
And ma black-eyed beauty
feeds me skin cornbread.

We'll eat eggs and bacon and turnip greens
in ma woody log cabin
in Ogen, Tennessee.

We'll travel again to Waco town
past the muddy Rio Grande
to the Lulu Club.

We'll hear the hot music from Africa land
and see the Zulu girls
do a black man's dance.

Imma traveling down the southern tracks.
Imma eats chocolate puddin'
and ma freight car's black

Imma traveler come to Rampart Street
And Imma walks miss Fanny
On Bourbon Street

Imma hungry hobo ridin' over this land
listening to the jazz
of the clack-clack night."

In My Rags

I saw a prostitute in front of a mirror
in a long purple wedding dress
and I wondered if she knew
it once belonged to a virgin.

I saw a bum in a suit at the thrift store
and I wondered if he knew it once belonged to a banker.

I saw a little girl wearing her Auntie's old swimming cap
and I wondered if she knew her Auntie had drowned.

I saw a soldier at the bar who cried
over the people he had to kill

and I wondered If he knew
he never had to go to war.

I sang a song to a deaf beggar
and wondered if he knew
the words were about him.

I saw a beggarman.

who drank from a chalice of silver and gold.

I wondered if he knew it had belonged to a king.

Piano Player

Too many times the piano player
played the same song over and over
as if she'd played it never before…
as if she knew no other tune…
until her only followers seemed to be
herself in an empty room;
and her piano would play evermore.

So many times she sang the same words
in the same way every day,
as if she knew no other songs-
until they floated away,
one by one, and no one
seemed to listen anymore.

Yet every day a young man stood
alone in the hallway
applauding her every note in his heart
as though each chord he heard
were a new sound to his ears,
hoping she would play it once more.

Rainbows in the Night

I see rainbows in the night,
I find starlit paths uncovered.
I listen to the silence of darkness
And the crackling of the fire.
A meteor streams across the sky.
The snows of yesterday have fallen
And softly cover these trails in white.
I walk them cautiously
Like a high wire act of bravery
through the forest's briny thickets.
Unfriendly noises follow behind
as I walk unguided like a pioneer,
not heeding the little dangers that be.
These are just the omens of a new journey,
and they do not vanish from my mind
nor does the unkindness they foretell.
Yet tuning back is a choice no more.

Statues of Stone

I dedicate these statues of stone
To each of the gods so many worship.
    Eros with an arrow to a lovers heart
      And wings for love's passing passions,
And Venus, the counterpart, in all Eros does
Stand together along the esplanade.
    Mars happily battles Ares, side by side.
And in another part of this mythical Earth,
Odin and Thor and Loki stand alone,
Flowers of worshipers tossed at their feet.
    What we do not know we fill in with gods
      To teach ourselves impossible lessons
    To believe and entrust to our souls.
        Moses parted a sea that parts itself every year.
        Lazarus, who never died rose from the dead.
Thousands sated themselves on 5 fish and a loaf of bread
(of course they did) and a prophet gravely injured
Rose from the dead with bleeding hands.
    In a lake where rocks stand just below water level
    He stepped from one rock to another,
    And they exclaimed, "Look! He walks on water!"
    I don't need to hear these tales anymore.

Look Up At Me

Look up at me my sad little love
Pretend for now all men are not alike
When I look down upon your beautiful face
Listening to the evening's grace
I see your golden eyes glistening with tears

So sad they have gained love's cruelest face
In the aftermath of separation
Like a sword dividing a cake down the middle
Suddenly everything created falls apart
Once a loving embrace now a broken heart

A hundred times he said he would never leave you
Every time you heard it you said I believe you
Now the crumbs of your love are strewn on the table
And no way to put them back together
Unable to understand how a man can be so fickle

Now you are a tree barren without leaves
Subject to the whims of the cold, the wind and rain
But know your leaves will someday return
But not the same ones who spurned you....
not the ones you wish to see again

My French Verses

When I read the French verses of Baudelaire
As they correspond with the English translation
I do so with my invented French accent
(only recognizing a few familiar French words).
 I imagine a Frenchman would laugh at me
As I destroy the language with a strange tongue.

Someday I will understand my own voice
As if the translations did not exist,
And I will go to Paris where poets abound
And hear my poetry destroyed with a French accent,
All meant with good intentions and love.

It would be dangerous to quote Rimbaud thus;
Then I would be open to his type of bad response.
(I'm not ready for my poetry to be toilet paper...or worse).

If I Were Mute

If I were mute I would want to be heard;
I would yell, scream or lecture; I'd be an orator.
>   If my tears were dammed my eyes would
>   Burst with tears. I would weep with joy.
If I were deaf I would seek out the loudest music
And every word of every conversation.
I would want to hear a baby cry and the birds coo.
>   If I were blind I would want to see the flowers,
>   The trees and the wonders of the world.
If I could not feel my fingers would reach out
To touch every thing I encountered.
>   If I could not walk I would want to run
>   Until I could go no further and finally dropped.
If my heart could no longer beat
I would want to live forever.

Tangled verses

I've read your verses
of tangled pain
in stanzas terse
with rhymes insane

your pictures framed
in old beliefs
before the romans came
to watch you in your grief

you rest beside the open gate
of sorrow's sad image
of torture and hate
laid upon the poet's page

no angel of any god
comes to lift you up and away
but leaves you bound in nature's pod
unhearing of what you say

the verses rime no more
nor clutch the visions lost
to tortures suffered before
with death the final cost

To The Poet Who Cried For Sylvia

Find the source
of pain in your head.
There's no reason
 to wish yourself dead.

Sylvia will wait forever
in endless time
while you finish
your faithful rimes.

Life is sometimes longer
than it should be.
Do it for yourself, do it for her:
it's free.

The tides always crest
above our abilities,
But surviving the waves
is our validity.

Journey From Africa (For Maya)

Washing away the plight of the journey
In order to see it in the light of history
Which took the people out of the past
Across the Devil's sea to this land
Of torment, humility and slavery

Then after centuries in the fields
Suffering the yokes of oppression
To be freed by those who enslaved
Thrust into a new age of opportunity
With the oppression of the chains gone
But both hatred and ignorance still enslaving.

There's the choice of poverty to remain in the fields.
But assailed by the whips of prejudice
And left to manage by pride and a lost music
Lodged in the mind's fond memories.

Or to escape to the cities of the cold north
Where nothing was familiar or home
Where the dirt of the fields are cobblestones
Leading to shacks made of brick and mortar
The homeland forgotten in jazz and blues

This is the history of the muse of Africa
Embraced in proud ceremony and dance.
Heard everywhere across this new land

In the alleys and backroom clubs
 From New York to Chicago to New Orleans.

Yet today you speak of tender things
As though all had been forgiven
In exchange for a peaceful harmony
That doesn't truly exist
Except in rhymes which are soon forgotten.

Ode to a Burro

The shed in the field stands empty
With carrot wreaths on its walls.
With teary notes on them all.
Her brush hangs from the fence

Where she'd lived her years
In the middle of this old gold rush town
Being fawned over by tourists,
But shouting her loudest bray for friends.

We brought her apples and carrots and hay
And always stopped to whisper in her ear.
She stood still for hand grooming
And fingers to comb her mane;

I hear in my memory her sweet bray.
The miners lettuce grows thick and wild now
And the little field blooms empty and green.
But there's no happy tail to shoo the flies away.

Sometimes There Are Dreams

Sometimes there's no reason

for the seasons to change

except to rearrange the forests,

or change the color of the ground

or to make heard the sounds

that echo through the trees.

there are times I lay awake

dreaming in awe

of the silent beauty of it all.

just as there are dreams

that lead to changes

as we re-arrange

the puzzle that appears,

because it isn't the same picture on the box.

yet, in the end,

it is the clearest picture of all.

Who Paints the Skies

Who do you think paints the skies
in reds and blues and amber hues?
Who do you think paints the reflections
on the rippled waters below?
All that work must be done at night
for I've never seen this artist at work.
Yet it is always there in the morning,
bright and rising and aglow.
And in the evening red and dark and yellow.
With the artist asleep beyond the clouds.

The Canvas

Upon the canvas of this page
Are the images I call my own.
I try vainly to see their meanings
In the mystery that is thought.

Strewn across this open canvas
Are the markings of lost visions
Enlightened slightly by the presence
Of these emotions
Stamped upon this page as you find them.

I push the rhythm of this brush
Until the canvas is full.
It is the strokes of the pen
Which make the images clear
In forms more familiar to you
Than these simple words can express.

If you come closer to the center of the canvas
Your eyes can capture them all.
Just as the musician's strings always
Bring feelings of warmth to your soul.
Now these images are yours, not mine.

To Those Lovers

you had your time together
but the adventure was not here.
the adventure was the journey to here.

and after all the explorations ended
and the harshness of reality descended
upon your pressing addiction to love's afflictions
you looked away from the promised path
in different directions with the pain of damaged souls
trading goals tarnished by love's tragedies-
and looking away from each other's eyes.

Paint a Picture Baby Jane

Paint a picture baby jane
Paint a picture of your shame
Let the world see what you've done
Tell them how you've strayed

Throw back your hair
Throw back your arms
Show them you're not afraid
Let them share the blame
See if anyone cares

I'm sure they've done the same
Its only a lover you've betrayed
Paint your picture baby jane
Paint a picture of your shame
Let your tears fall in vain.

Tribute To Haiti

I want to believe I'll once again hear
the sounds of happy musicians
playing silly melodies
as the children dance and sing.
Some psychedelic raindrops
from another day long ago
come washing away the blur of today
into the ash cans of this tragedy.
I am reminded to remember
to reminiscence about what once was
in order to believe what I see now.

Yet now is unbelievable.
It unfolds before my eyes
as these daily tragedies
manifesting themselves
with overwhelming force.

More than Hiroshima
and more than Nagasaki.
These man-made tragedies of war
Don't compare to nature's devastations.
Unlike the holocausts of history
perpetrated over years
these events occur in seconds
with instant results of lasting carnage.

Everywhere the raindrops of history
are wiped away like yesterday's tears
and turned into instant fears
of this Earth's almighty powers.

Walking through the stench
and not recognizing the dead
does not halt the loss I feel
nor close the pain inside

Yet recognizing a mother,
a sister and a son or father,
all screaming at the sky for an answer,
brings no resolution in this rubble.

The tents are full
and shanties rise from the ash

while grasshoppers hide
for fear of being a meal.

The Voodoo doctor with his magic
performs his sacred rites
as Christians steal the children
to sell them into a different life.

This island swims between
poverty and death
surrounded by an angry sea
and resting on a shaking earth.

In crumbling bricks and thatch,
the screams and whimpers
of dying and broken survivors
call out the names of children lost.

Subway Funny Dream

everyone is going away
running away
riding the subway trains
with frozen hands
In their pockets
leading them nowhere
they want to be
as they ride
and ride and ride
away from everything
in their heads
and leave me here
with no way to find
a make-believe world
to live in.

down now
this tripping train is slowing
to a place where birches bend
to shake their leaves away
and the wind blows them off to war
floating past my windows,
they go off to wars,
marching off to wars
of new forms flowing
and drumming
down the city's avenues
as this nightmare dreams on.
resting my mind in the open arms
of this insane dream I dream
makes my spirit wonder why
I hold to these visions
so desperately.

it's a quiet time
of bedtime rhymes
even as the sun shines
upon so many daytime rhymes
and the words and words,
so many words
that flow through this mind

and make my times of rhyming.
so quietly prevailing.

disillusion unveils the mime
of sliding through the wonders
and riding thunderous
through the sky
with so much lost
in each rhyme.

a desolate sheet of eerie designs
glows brightly and warm
in this fantasy of make believe
where fireplace embers burn red
long after the flames have disappeared.
this warmth flows through my soul
as my yearnings sleep
and I ride this subway funny dream
into a strange and foreign world.
many floors to lay on
and many cages to scream from
as I roll inside this stone
cascading downward
o'er mossy green grasses
wetted by the foggy mists of night.

I travel astride a red fawn
kicking aside
the logs of fallen oaks
strewn wildly in my path.

        I am listening to
        the woodsmen chipping
        and hear the trees fall far away
        as I look back and wonder
        where all my subways
        could have gone.

        licorice likeness is the night
        I travel through
        and chimney wastes
        are my licorice tastes.
        my licorice tears
        softly touch my fears

Denmark

In Denmark,
which is really not a land,
But a place I've never been,
A thousand yellow winged birds
Sing daily songs
to throngs of dolphins
Who hang possum-like from the branches of trees
And sway gently with the breeze of melodies
Coming from these foreign beaks

Although these dolphins are never certain
Of the meanings to the songs they hear
In brushing carelessly against the trees
They seem enthralled merely by the rhapsody,
And needless care to know
the philosophies
Behind which these birds are singing
In complete harmony of voice.

(Moved probably by their ability to fly
and somewhat by a desire not to die alone.)

But Denmark is really not a land,
but simply just a place
 I've never been.

Somewhere A Lark

somewhere a lark
or possibly some other bird
with a better name
might sit on a branch and
sing about the toys the children play with
or break, which is also a game,
in the country back yards of their city homes,
with a few weeds for a field
and a dirt pile for a mountain.
or if he is a better bird,
or a lark with a shorter tail,
he might fly away and look for acorns
in real trees
in a forest where Nobody has ever been.
and, unless Nobody takes a shot at him,
he can fly back and drop the acorn
in the child's backyard and
wait until after he is old to watch it
grow into some marvelous tree
which the child,
by then an old wreck of a human being,
will not be able to climb
and probably too blind to see,
unless some miracle of medicine
has rendered him forever a child,
which, of course, you and I know
is highly improbable if not unlikely.

I See People

I see people floating like dreams
O'er the open streets of the world
Filling the picture-puzzle spaces
Of emptiness with the visions
Of each one.

Beneath the clouds the stars the meteors
And the planets humans mill about
Building their own worlds with their dreams
Filling those spaces with new wonders
And an earthly universe only to destroy it
And themselves over and over again
Constantly reinventing themselves
Setting the stage to repeat all
Of their past mistakes

Heather Hay

Heather hay of yesterday
with little feet that children greet
in Chelsea town and county down
brings to mind all memories kind.

Send me new fantasies
so I can write their inner dreams
that seem so bright and full of realities
yet leave me here imprisoned.

Don't let me see these bars
Or feel these concrete walls
But let it all disappear
Into the fantasies of my mind.

Let me be deaf to the tortured sounds
And blind to the riots of rage
Which spin all about this cage
While I roam inside this mind.

She Wanders Alone

In the morning she walks
and wanders alone
from coffeehouse to café,
texting friends who might read
her daily mutterings.
She jots down her poetry
In her little blue book.
No one walks with her
And no one sits at her side.
At the end of the day she walks home alone
To wait for answers to her calls.

From This Window

I think I can write again
in this place I have settled.
I can look out through the trees,
with no bars to confine my view
or block out my thoughts of the sun.

The past comes ever to mind
and ignoring it is not easy.
Outside, smoke drifts from the chimney
and a light breeze carries it away,
disappearing into the mountain's forest.
The morning dew has left
every leaf dripping.
I think this is the place
where I might resurrect the muse

Humankind

I am studying this strange thought
of humankind, captured
by its own creations.
And there is the thought
of the seething masses
of concrete erections
all built in a row
with the people
milling about
these monuments
and looking back
at what they've left behind.

There Was a Time

in the winter of this journey
 we find each other.
when I'd almost forgotten
your smiling face.
I'd not forgotten your grace
and the way you smell.
I never forgot your sweet embrace
 or your touch.
I remember the sweet softness of your hair.
Your smile touched my deepest emotions.
There were those days apart,
and then the days of suffering.
Was it that way for you
or am I just selfish and weak?
But now those feelings have vanished
with you here again.
It is better I've forgotten the past
 so I can enjoy today.

Alligators

coming down the open road
to the shady everglades and swamps
I stop to watch the alligators
digging holes to bury their victims.
while my heart strains
at this carnivorous planting

I find it amusing to watch them make their ditches
in the black and soggy soil
and clumsily stomp back to their everglade
hiding places to probably await me.

so I remain here on the road
where I can walk safely past these everglade traps
where lay this gargantuan beast of water and land,
and that way avoid its waiting with wisdom.

I am content for sure it will not starve,
though my own limbs I will not give
nor offer by mistake.

Spirits in the night

We are never alone in the night.
The night is there to comfort us.
There is solitude in the soul.
There are many souls in these nights.

My Sidartha

You live.
You have great moments
and bad moments,
you suffer love and hate,
and you age.
You get sick and you die.

You do it all while tied to the earth
and its greater cosmos.
Do it with grace
and forgiveness.
Don't do what you hate
to others
and it will all
be worthwhile.

Colors

Red white black brown and yellow we blend
Into a nation split by all those things
and the lost memories of those who suffered
or offered upon us great harm
Yet through it all we did not flee or bend
We are fractured by opinions which do not matter
And torn by the lower hatreds that still exist today
But trudge forward as if there were a happy ending
In the future of our splintered lives
With blinders firmly planted o'er our eyes

Concert

The fairgrounds full of tie-dyed shirts
wandering about their compound alleys of
Rasta vagabond painted buses
and their tents and bare feet in rags
with platters of psychedelic medicines
passed all around
edging nimbly through this city of abandon.
all the people walking in slow motion before me
I see nothing but smiles in the midst of this maze.
But from fantasy to civilization I have to go.

Travels With Izzy

Traveling through these rolling hills,
we sing all the songs we know.
This is where boulders and rocks
push upwards from the
California clay.
I wonder if these stones were planted here
by a gardener with a sense of humor.
Crossing the bridge over the river
near Mark Twain's ancient cabin,
"Let's hope he's home,' jokes Izzy.
"We should stop by and see first hand.
Perhaps his soul is still wandering about
or maybe his muse is sitting inside by the fire".
But nothing is there for our make-believe,
just an old wooden cabin enshrined
inside a chain link fence.
So we drive away toward Angels Camp,
where the story of his frogs lives on today,
singing the songs we know so well.

My Maine Coon

The softness of my Maine Coon
I could compare to nothing else
not to a baby's skin
nor the illusiveness of china silk.
the softness of her purr
is a murmur in the night.
she curls up warm and close in bed
for all the night ahead.

Once I saw her sitting on Papa's table,
still alive today, though he is gone and dead,
she still able to fill this heart with warmth
while he no longer fills his page with romance.

I saw her dancing with an angel in my dream
both swirling around to the music of another time
while I watched alone
unable to touch either one.

As he passed by

He saw them standing down the road,
milling about idly in a deep yellow field.
as he drew close and each appeared
He felt and saw their fates abandon.

"How far have you traveled?" He heard one ask.
"I've come from across the Universe only
 to find you waiting without a place to go."
One by one they nodded as he passed by.

They had stepped away as he walked through,
and yet he'd asked none of them to yield.
They fell behind as he walked away.
and he heard the quiet rumble of their voices.

One called to him, "How much have you seen?"
"I've seen too much and forgotten even more."
"Now I find you've lost your ways."
And each one nodded as he passed by.

He wondered why no one asked if he had lost his dreams
and he could only think of how far he'd come.
It was not long after he heard their footsteps fade away,
his calloused soles scraping the dusty path.

The vision of their gathering remained in his thoughts.

Those people he'd come upon stranded in that field

were not the first he had encountered along this road.

And they would not be the last.

Elves

I really don't know what to do
with these elves you've sent me in a shoe.
They're almost too short for me to see.
And, of course, it would have been better
if you'd have sent them in a letter.
Then, when I peeked inside,
I could take them out and set them aside.
Why, I could've put them in my secret drawer
or even given them to someone poorer.
I know I don't need more than what I've got.
Perhaps they could all be taken out and shot.
But that would not be a very nice thing to do.
Maybe I should simply take them all to the zoo,
Except I think they wouldn't like that at all:
They'd rather, I think, go shopping at the mall.

Lyrics

he loved her in the morning
and he loved her again at night,
but something came between them
and it just didn't seem right.
Her smile was different
then when they met that first day
and her eyes had lost their glow.
And her touch had lost its' warmth
Yet he loved her just the same
as she walked out the door.
Now that she is gone,
he loves her even more.

Ode To Mr. Poe

The fortune teller reads the stars
and tries to tell us who we are.
It's no secret, Mr. Poe,
how you've amused yourself
and kept your mind the way it is.
But you may have ventured a bit too far
for the fortune tellers to read your signs.
for you, my friend, that's enough for now.
though you are engrained in every line I write,
sought by Poeters and poetesses, unlike the others,
you are the same in every verse you wrote.

The Pit

The pit that has engulfed you,
this abyss of silence that takes you away,
leaves me standing at the edge
to watch you disappear.

I can't follow you into nowhere
or jump in after you in vain.
I must stand alone and know
you might never return again.

There is sadness in my heart
each time you come to mind.
It must be sadness who writes these songs,
for it's not right for laughter to cry.

A keg of beer

a keg o' beer,
a vat 'o wine,
a small batch o' shine,
a woman to hold,
friends to throw rocks at,
a dog to blame,
and a carriage to sleep in.
this is all I ask

It Is Late

It is late.
The garden is asleep.
The horses are in the barn.
The geese make noises at shadows.
The moon watches over the clouds.
Sleep will come easy tonight.

Dawn

dawn is lighting up the night;
by morning it will be alright.
time waits for tomorrow to arrive
to see if yesterday is still alive.

And kiss the sun

and some day
after the people have gone
and the houses have crumbled
to the ground,
I will walk
this soil
among the grasses
the trees
and the fields.

I will sweep the plains
with my ripened thought
and swim the waters
with my opened soul.

I will stand upon
the mountains high
to embrace the skies
and kiss the sun.

Dreams

It could be almost anything
It could be when the moon was full
Or when you fell in love that time
Or when you lost your mind.
You never know about dreams
Until they come to light
In the middle of the night
To be forgotten in the fog of day.

Lovers

The days are gone now of the open road.
the music has faded beyond these travels.
And in the past now, this list of lovers.
I remember their touch, their hair,
The way they spoke
and the way they smelled.
I may have forgotten their names.
But one stood out like no other.
Still, I struggle with her name.

Empty Soul

The mind is filled with a whole life:
everyone you have ever known,
everything you have ever done
and every memory of every event of your life.
But don't let worry or regret close your eyes
and empty your soul.
When you look past these things,
your eyes open and you can see once more,
and you are full again.

Watching it end

I've seen the ancient fortress fall into the sea.
I've seen the winds bring mountains down.
I've even touched the clouds in the sky.
I've seen the beginning and the in-between
And I'm waiting for it to end.

The Stream

no matter how many boulders there are in the stream,
the water will always flow around and through them.
I read this thought to a man about the stream
but he said he could only see the boulders.

We Are Never Alone

We are never alone
We can always argue with our thoughts
We can dream of days with friends in the past
We have our souls to punish us
We have our hearts to reward us

Greeting The Rain

I aspire to greet the rain in the morning.
The gains that are lost in this life
Are regained in the after-life.
It warps my brain to think of it.
After a night awake in dreaming
I let the moonlight sleep it's sleep.
And in the morn I greet the rain.

Drums

Good ones are played in the heart.
Why are you beating
your drums so loud?
You make the clouds tremble
with your noise.
Who needs to hear your noise
If you can't hear it yourself?
Bad messages are told with drums.

Asphalt

asphalt meeting concrete
loitering city boys
with all their toys
railroad tracks and selling crack
in plastic sacks to baby jacks
in Cadillacs cruising through the hood
all misunderstood

yellow bridge across the river
homeless tents below
backstreet alleys
broken lives
litter in the park
no place to go but here
no children to be seen

sirens screaming
tempers streaming
gunshots in the night
the city is not right

homeless camped on
hard sidewalks in cardboard houses
as far as the eye can see

Did you hear Death has died?

I am the wind that sweeps the land
and my name to you is Death.
You don't know where I come from,
though you try to map my progress.
You build wind-towers of wood and tin
and you say to your neighbor,
"The wind blows from the east."
And all is well 'til I twist about
and pluck your neighbor from their bed
with the west wind behind my back.

The poets and philosophers
have tell you who I am:
they say I am the long sleep,
the final rest and the end to it all.
The reward for a life of hard work and toil
in a world of uncertainty and question.
This is what the poets have said.

But, what if I, Death, were to die?
What if the wind stopped and the land was calm?
What if nobody, anywhere, heard my name?
Have you ever asked yourself that?

Would you sit there on your carpenter porches
and whisper little gossip to each other,
"Did you hear that Death has died?

"Yeah, and now they want to bury her
in the fields that heard her voice
and on the plains that heard her cries."

Then you'd want to tear down the wind-towers
because they never worked in the first place.

And where would you bury Death?
Who would dig the hole to gently slide her into,
and who would build the redwood casket,
and how big do you think it should be?

I mean to say, if I had been this good to you
over all these years of steadily working-
if I was what the poets say I am-
don't you think you would owe me something more
than just the evening gossip of

"Did you hear that Death has died?"

The Towne Crier

And in my mornings waking
I hear the town crier
riding o'er the cobblestones
of my thought
and approaching my gates
 in the realm of my dreams
and asking the time
of my weary soul.

I tell him it is midnight
inside my dreams
and he turns with his stead
away from my gates
and shouts to the town
of people in waiting
that it is midnight,
and all is well.

Ode To Masefield

So thar yer layin', John Masefield,
All buried in the deep.
Yer gone an' left us all
And yer 'heart 'as 'eard its beat.
But I'll tell yer this, me friend,
Yer no been cheated from yer song.
I'd just grown to likin' it
An' I'll love it afore too long.
Now yer awares, me 'opes,
That our father were the same.
'e lived seven hundred years ago
An' Chaucer were 'is name.
So yer gone away, John Masefield,
An just as well it is.
For yer lived a lovin' life
An' eighty- eight's too long for bliss.
So's I kiss yer grave
An' walks me way,
Thinkin' of the songs yer gave
An' the long, long time it's been.

(Friday, May 12, 1967, upon an icon's death))

The Devil's Coach

I blew across the skies on a riderless mare
into the winds of tomorrow' cries
and left the footprints of my dreaming cares
on the broken panes of godless time.

I left behind a heart full of children
to follow ambition to the gates of Hell
and found my journey stopped in the Garden of Zen
where monks sat musing my words and rhyme.

I took with me my priceless trinkets in brass
donated by friends wearing weeds and moss
but had everything stolen by a two-legged ass
while stranded in the midst of a waterless pond.

I stayed briefly in the rippled land of flesh
to fondle with emotion the limbs of love
and received those caresses in jest
from the womb of a lover of whom I was fond.

I traveled back through this journey
upon the wings of an oaken sailing ship
and discovered gold in the sea of departure
after battling it out with the Captain of Death.

I rested at last on the plains of grassy fortune
only to find myself sucked under the ground
by the strumming sounds of the clock's bad tunes
and heard in my sleep the reaper's approach.

I fought for my life in the forest of lost dreams
with the young swordsmen of hate and revenge
and saw my heart plucked out by Simon Peter
who touched my wet lips as I took my last breath.

I watched in helpless wonder the circling clouds
in darkening skies above my head
and rose to the marching trumpets playing loud
the dirge of the Devil as I entered his coach.

She Sips Her Cherry Brew

She tripped softly through the diamond fields
and ran floating o'er the plains of yellow grass.
She passed slowly her leaping cadences
o'er the mountain's snowy paths.

She dank thirstily from the running waters
tumbling down beside her.
She came into this world already wise
and grew into her years of wisdom's thought.

She married the seas to carry her off
and gave rubies to her many ships.
A marshmallow heaven entered her heart
and her soul reached out to embrace
a world of purple fantasy.

Her arms held the lovers she loved forever
and her lips kissed the children playing in the park.
Her mother shouted loud her not forgiving love
while her father raped her innocent soul.

Her brother took her body
and built his cherry tree land.
Her sister fondled with jealousy
her fantasies of poetry and peace.

She gave to all she met
a glowing smile of welcome,
and to her everyday man,
she gave secrets of hidden dreams.

She made her bed of lavender flowers
in a life of brutal charms
and she drank her cup of living
in her world of soft regret.

She played her gold-stringed harp
in the dying fields of grass
and ran deftly though the forest
and held her lovers with trembling hands.

She opened every door she faced
and gave her heart to all.
She felt the glory of her life
in giving it her dreams.

Now she sits alone
on the evening porches of her age
watching silently
those who passed through her life.

Now she sings her quiet songs
to lovers gone and past
and remembers the years of open fields
and sips her cherry brew.

Yellow Giant Bird

I have dreamed of dying yellow plants,
all topped and eaten by grey little ants,
who kill my gardens but open my arms
with loves and girls and boyish charms.

I have imagined a cylinderic atmosphere
of empty happenings and tempered tears
in the many years of my Plato gods
who suck on berries and plough the sod.

I have hallucinated dreams of reality
In the purple womb of charity
which gave my mind a hollow mold
of green trees ripening in days of old.

I have invented lovers and held their hands
And planted my house on shifting sands,
only to watch it fall and kiss its' death
and utter within a warming breath.

I have created a poetry of sillowed colors
in controlled ragings of rampant splendor
that catch my love and tear its cloth
like a yellow giant bird eating a moth.

I have dreamed a fantasy land of bubbles
which pop up red and eat their troubles

like a magistrate without his magic gavel
to pound and change his judgements to gravel.

I have listened to the night time
and heard the day with its oddly rhyme.
I've caught the flying birds of my mind
And sent them home with their sorted kinds.

I have spoken of sharpened thought and idea
in stripping the clothes of my golden Medea
so I could see her body in naked light
and drown these oceans of Plutonic plight.

I have smelled the summer's yellow flowers
grown in the night to enlighten my hours
of days and years of dreaming alone
  to the remnants of lovers postponed.

I have touched the thoughts of my dreams
and felt the softness of all fantasies seem
to touch the muscles of my stomach
which flex in tautness and shrivelic aches.

I have tasted the universe without praying
to the gods of merciless cravings
and spit the blood of tubercular hobbies
in the pillars of these marbled lobbies.

I have seen the ending to all this journey
flow into the past like a jostled tourney
of Knights and Ladies and girls and boys
who fight to suppress their trivial joys.

I have happened the experienceable
in the transient world of the impossible
with the wondering fables of wandering
through the mind of all my quandaries.

I have fought the battle of the dying lad,
who at last seeing death may not be so bad,
is finally glad to feel his brother's hand
leading him away to a new-born land.

I've loved the dreams of all these whirls,
and felt the arms of translucent red curls
in the old land of the improbable dreams
that clutched my dreaming elastic seams.

I have ended and gone and left and come
to this plain of tundra beating drums
in the vastness of Antarctica
where all dreams grow in replica.

I have thought a billion untold thoughts
and suffered within the terror they've brought
in my endless trampling of realities dread
and this mind's stampede to an empty bed.

I have nightmares in my sleepless days
in the light of the moon's happy play
among the sea fishes eating octopi,
and said hello to my frightened good-byes.

I have written of dreaming sexualities,
of bodies molded in voided trivialities,
who take the hand of the devious to squander
and unfold the skies where the night bird wanders.

I have thought the thought of procreation
in the midst of mankind in devastation,
seeking one's brother and killing one's parents
in the blackening fog of end-time transparent

I have heard the news from the murdered politics
and the meaningless cravings of the old fanatics
who stumble the everyday same road
like a pond full of colorless blind toads.

I have died in the evening's birthday
and risen in the tomorrow of yesterday
to destroy the plans of truculent haters
and bury the rules of sick-time shakers.

I have come, I have gone, and I stand between
What is left and remains now clandestine
in the labyrinth of my memories maze
of all else that leaves or strays.

I have, at last, sung all these songs
and searched my mind for the universal wrong
that has always traveled with us before
as I wait for the answers that lie in store.

The Death of Simeon Adele

finally looking backward
from his deathbed,
Simon Adele stole his visions of life
as if to take them with him
and mixed them in his memory
and packed them in his imaginary bags.

and these events which led backward to his birth
in a swift and frightful flit of years
were twisted 'round in his mind
as he watched them quickly peak in time until
they lapped at last like the northern ocean
splashing down on his deathbed sheets
and drowning the nurse in waiting,
who stood beside him with his temperature
rising wildly in her hands.

Greenland

What a funny little wooden ship this is,
sailing with the clouds,
as it follows a sternward wind
into its own foggy dream
searching for tomorrow and now.

Eric Rauda in 974,
with icicles breaking
off his bright red beard,
shouts out to his crew an order
only they can understand.

"We'll travel to the western worlds
and rape below the mainsails
all those we shall encounter."

This ship, bouncing up and down,
and through and above
these clouds and waves,
until all is calm
upon this ragged sea.

Barnacles snag and tow
the scattered grand octopi
who live below this ship's journey,
and the captain's cabin

fills with the smells of mead.
Then all the drunken sailors,
stripped naked to their toes,
run wildly across this slippery deck
of icy wooden cards,
seeking games to hide in.
There are no hooks
to hang their clothes or heads upon.

And from the galley comes
the shout of the cook's apron,
"Harpoon the full speed ahead
and send me another boy for the stew."

A bubbling, babbling, bobbing ship;
this funny little ship we sail.
Full of naked and hungry sailors,
traveling westward o'er this ocean of clouds
in search of another world within this world.

Pushed onward by the cold, cold winds of chance,
are the unknown gods of Greenland's icy coast,
making conjugations for their splendid forms.

But finding ports may fail
and leave these adventurers adrift in the wind.
Below, the pious seashells mix a magic brew
to feed these drunken sailors
and lead them to their journey's end.

How odd, this funny little ship.
 How odd, indeed, these sailors, too.
Upon the ship's decks
they grow strange potions
to hang across the bow,

and in the chill of the winds
they find their sanities again.
Following flocks of geese flying home,
like feathered compasses
silhouetted by the moon's happy face,

they are on their way to a place
they've never seen before.
There they can melt
 the floral iceberg from below
and sail above it's northern shores.

It's on this funny ship they roam,
a potted plant upon the seas,
where the cook in his apron
can boil away his wicked stew.

Then comes the cry from the crow's nest,
"Land Ho!
 And soon, steady as she goes,
a place to port comes near-
a place to shout a mighty cheer.

Now these hungry sailors gather
about a handsome fire
on the shores of a green land
they never knew could exist
until they heard the captain's orders
so many, many days before.

And each one shivers in the cold
and hangs his clothes to dry.

But there is no one to greet them,
no women to plant their sails in,
no natives to battle or meet them,
just the birds they had followed
and the octopi peeled from the bow.

It was then Greenland sank from sight
and Eric Rauda cried out,
"Wail, little ship!
Your tale is told".

They now must all return.
They've plundered the shores
of this green land,
and found nothing to guide them home.

The masts are torn. Their souls are worn,
yet they must return once more,
to search these sands for their rewards,
like the naked sailors they are."

The Homeless Promenade

Not now, my sweet,
but some other time,
we'll meet for breakfast
at the bistro by your place.
And yes, you can bring your little dog.
And, of course, I'll bring mine.

We'll take a walk down the promenade,
arm in arm, like the old days.
Except now, we'll be dignified about it.
We'll take our time with our little strays.
They'll think we've made the grade.

But not now, my sweet. we'll have to wait for spring.
You'll wear the old blue dress
You wore the day we met.
I'll wear my ragged, yellow suit
and they'll all be impressed.
They'll think we've got the world on a string.

Oh, and bring your umbrella.
You can loft it on your shoulder very proud.
You can twist it with your fingers
and make it twirl round and round.
I'll bring the walking cane I carved in the park
and you should wear your string of pearls.

We'll be so grand once again.
I'll wear a piece of linen for a scarf
while I give my cane a spin.

You can wear your old felt bonnet,
so there's no need to fix your hair.
And you should wear
those high heeled shoes
you found beneath the stairs.

They made you seem so much taller
and together we'll be a pair.
We'll be just two happy lovers
who've forgotten all their cares

I'm sure we can survive
their hoots and hollers
when they see us walk on past.
I'll even shine my boots.
And, if anyone asks,
we'll give them our autographs.

Perhaps we'll pause and I'll tip my hat.
I'm sure they'll all love that.
Some will say we're two old clowns
playing dress-up for some praise.
We'll be the talk of the town
when we have our little parade.

It'll be just like the old days
when we were young and alive.
They will never believe
how dignified we are.

But not now, my sweet,
we'll have to wait
for the rain to go away.

The Frenchman in the Garden

Why is there a Frenchman in the garden,
Is he busy searching for escargot?
He stands erect like a well-trained mime,
When anyone can see he's not a statue?
Except, the birds seem to pay him some mind.

The snow is melting all around his feet,
and drips on his head from the juniper tree,
He stands so straight without a smile.
I can tell he takes it too seriously.

I'd like to invite him in for some tea
to spare him the farce of this predicament.
But he seems quite content with his plight.
though it may seem right to offer him a tent.

For the meantime, I'll just draw the curtains
and hope when they open he'll have gone away.
I'll forget all about the Frenchman in the garden
and get back to my duties before I fall astray.

But that doesn't erase his image in my mind,
nor does it allow me to get back to my work.
So I open the curtains and yell out the window,
"Get out of my garden. Have you gone berserk?"

Questions for A Traveler

So what else did you rattle on
and what else did you see?
Did you follow a nimble ship
And cast away to sea?

Did you eat your morning seaweed
and bask upon the deck?
Did you come upon an island
or have a deathly wreck?

So tell me at my side once more
the trip you sailed last night.
And tell me all about the girls
with whom you had delight.

(Or were there only gravely men
inside that dream you went?)
And tell me what has happened there
that makes you now so bent.

Tell me as I listen here
about your evening trip.
Tell me why you are bleeding
and why your clothes are ripped.

Tell me all about your journey
and where you left your smile.
Please tell me why you return so soon
and was it all worthwhile?

The Old Tree

I remember an old tree
that grew in the forest.
I leaned on it once
and it stood over there.

There's a special thing
about the forest-
Why, everywhere you look
there's a tree.

I remember an old tree
that grew over there.
But now I can see
someone has moved it.

Moving a tree is not
a normal thing to do,
especially if it was over there,
of all places.

You can see how confusing
this is to me.
Can anyone please
tell me where to look?

If you know who
moved the old tree and why,
that would be even better.

I'm asking you
because you are my friend
and I don't know anyone
else to ask but you.

I thought I couldn't see the tree
 for the forest,
but that's just an old saying
 I had heard.

I think for now I'll just go back
to my log cabin.
I'll close the oaken door
 and wait for your news.

The Old Captain

The old captain
 charts the seas
of his lost miseries
as though it's tides
will lead him to destiny's gates.

Mapping every jagged emotion
felt along the way,
he tries to predict
what future path might lay ahead.

But, the sea's winding path
stays in his mind
as he tries to recapture
the events
from his inglorious past.

Looking back across the departing land,
those events are gone.
They are as dried and as gone
as summer's sagging flowers in the fall.

Today's attack of the hourglass
is his unwelcome surprise.
His charts are lost
as the sand trickles
away his days.

The ocean's waves toss across
the bow of his ship.
The winds send him closer
to the sea's deep end.

Too bad, my sad captain.
it could have all been perfect.
The natives could have greeted you
upon their shores.

They could have taken you home
and shown you off.
They could have raised you up
and called you a god.

Instead, they had a better idea
of what to do with you.
They put you in a boiling pot
and prepared to make you stew.

Destiny's gates have been waiting
for your journey to end.
It finds you here still pondering
What your next move should be.

But that decision's now been made
in waters boiling hot.
There's nothing left for you to do
but cook inside your pot.

164

Letters to Lorraine

The Letters

Winter   1838

I have finished and the snow begins to fall.
I wish you a happy birthday in French.
Please don't tell me again you are old.
You are simply more beautiful than ever.

Before the winter came I put the birds away.
I could hear the animals howling at night.
I knew they'd soon come prowling.
The birds know why I've marched them inside.

It's hard to have you so far away for so long.
I miss your gentle touch and your warmth,
but always I imagine you here beside me.
That is what guides me through every day.

I have not written any new rhymes today.
I am torn over what I must write, yet cannot.
I would rather love you from a thousand miles
than spend my time in rhyming thought.

The snow is falling like a white blanket now.
All the trees are beginning to sag and droop
I love this time when the first snow falls.
It always reminds me of our first days here.

My new white goose follows me everywhere
I've named her Maggie and she is nice to hold.
She stands outside the cabin and watches me.
She must know we have much in common.

Say hello to the children and give them my love.
Tell Jacob to do his studies and not be a bore.
He knows he'll have to take my place one day.
Let Rachael know I'll send her a poem soon.

Spring   1839

Your letter came today and it made me smile.
The picture of you and the children is grand.
I'm glad that Rachael enjoyed her last rhyme.
Tell Jacob how proud I am of his good work.

I'm still splitting wood but winter's chill is gone.
The birds have multiplied like feathered rabbits.
I'll soon take the goslings to the auction house.
The older birds are grazing freely now.

I have been writing day and night for months.
Winter's kept my body in and sets my mind free.
You are always my inspiration and my muse.
I see and feel your aura in every line I write.

I'm writing to you by a warm evening fire.
I don't know how I tolerate your absence,
but the good of the children is best for us all.
I have not been working at my desk today.

It looks like Jacob is starting to grow taller.
Rachael's smile is so endearing. I miss them.
It has not been long, but it seems forever
since we were all here at home together.

I must go back to work or I'll get behind.
Sometimes when I think of you I lose my place.
Yet other times it forces me to work harder.
The white goose stands in the doorway now.

Tell Grammy Beth I send my love and gratitude.
I'll have some money soon to send you all.
And this time I'll write a poem for everyone.
I've set your picture upon my desk as company.

Summer 1839

I wait in anticipation for your letters each day.
I am happy everyone laughed at my last poem.
It's a good thing to have fun with my loneliness.
It's good to know the children have new friends.

I've kept your garden and it flourishes each day.
The field has dried and left the birds searching.
I'll ride to the granary today and buy them feed.
All the goslings are sold. They were sweet birds.

Your words have given me my comfort and joy,
even though you and the children are far away.
My words are flowing through my mind wildly.
This writing is starting to breath its own life.

I've seen a black wolf walking above on the hill.
He has settled in the shade of a tree by day.
He sees the birds and he sees me watch him.
Tonight, I'll put the birds away and load my musket.

This is wonderful. It has begun to rain as I write.
I suspect this downpour will not last very long,
but it's made the wolf leave for a better shelter.
There is so much I notice since you have gone.

I must put the birds away and go to the granary.
When I return I will go back to work once more.
These distractions help me keep my sanity.
Otherwise, I would likely die from laziness.

Let the children know how much I miss them.
I'll try to write something for them to laugh about.
The rain has stopped, just as I thought it would.
To all of you, and Grammy Beth, I send my love.

Fall 1839

It is quiet here, with a breeze softly blowing.
I am delighted to hear everything is going well.
The children's notes were a wonderful sight.
Their French improves so rapidly. I am proud.

The black wolf has returned to the hill above.
He worries me and he worries the birds, too.
They yell in the oddest way when he appears.
But the white goose always remains near

I am coming to the end as I write this chapter
It has been almost a year I've worked on this.
I think I would not be such a silly perfectionist,
if I didn't hear your voice in my mind as I write.

I think of you always as I try my best to finish.
Sitting by the fire you cannot escape my mind.
At my desk, my head throbs, waiting for words.
One by one, they drip like water from a spout.

The rising wind blows leaves past the doorway.
There may be a storm to keep me inside again.
It may be what it takes to make the words flow.
I've not heard the birds squawking today.

I've fallen asleep in the midst of this letter
and the leaves blowing in have wakened me.
I look outside and the wolf stands in the yard.
Maggie flutters her wings beside my desk.

He might not come back since I scared him off.
The birds are hiding but Maggie won't leave me.
I've made a nest in a box where she can sleep.
I send my love to you and the children and Beth

Andrew

Andrew arrived to visit at the cabin today.
He rode alone from the other side of the mountain.
It's been more than a year since he's ridden this far.
He was surprised to hear that you are all abroad.

He's very proud that he is fourteen now.
I asked if his father treats him as a man now.
He said, of course, when it comes to chores.
Andrew always had a good sense of humor.

Did you know he's as tall as Jacob now?
Today we hiked down the canyon to the creek.
We hopped rocks over the water for a ways,
finally   stopping at the swimming hole about noon.

We rested on the boulder in the pond
we dived off when we were young.
Andrew threw his clothes and dove in.
I shivered just watching him.

We sat for a spell while Andrew dried off in the sun,
and I asked him how his family were getting along.
Andrew always shakes his head when he's puzzled.
He was silent for some time and he shook his head.

I didn't expect tears. He had seemed so carefree,
but their land was taken by the British for taxes.
They've left and his father asks us to take him in.
Jacob would be heartbroken without him

I embraced him. I told him he was family to us.
I knew you wouldn't mind that I agreed right away.
I miss and love you all, until we are together again.
I hope what I've sent will last until the spring.

Maggie

Your letter arrives in the midst of a winter storm.
The children's notes in French are beautiful.
Andrew's so happy to hear from Jacob and Rachael.
He's been helpful and given me more time to work.

The wolf has not returned. Maggie stays close by.
The other birds stay close when we do the chores.
I expect he'll return again. I wonder what he wants.
Perhaps he has no pack and we are his only company.

Andrew sleeps in Jacob's bed. Maggie's in her crate.
They've both given me much needed company.
I've been assigned a new project for Le Poste.
I'm thinking of you each day with every line I write.

An image came to mind today as I rested from work.
I saw us as children playing; and then I saw us today.
In so many ways our feelings have never changed.
We have so much left to do and a lifetime to do it.

Snow is blowing hard now. Andrew is making a fire.
I always like the snow. It makes me work harder.
The trees are white and the birds have hunkered in.
For this project, I am describing our wilderness life.

I know you never allowed any birds inside the cabin.
You may change your rmind when you meet Maggie.
Andrew has taken to her, and they are friends.
She's stands on the doorstep fluttering her wings.

I hope you will send us another photograph soon.
I've enclosed some money so you can have one made.
In the spring, we'll have the family portrait done.
My heart is with you all and Andrew sends his love.

The Ojibwe

The rider who brings your posts is a frozen man.
This new photograph is as good as if you were here.
Andrew pinned Jacob's letter to the wall by his bed.
His art work is impressive and I've put it by my desk.

This morning we have seen the oddest behavior yet.
The birds are quiet, even when the wolf is close.
He has returned and he paces through the snow.
He makes his tracks around the tree on the hill.

An Ojibwa hunting party came visiting the other day.
They were happy with the gift of eggs and quills.
And they gave me a warm, otter skin turban.
They were most amused watching me put it on.

Four dogs pull their two toboggans, full of furs.
They stayed with us overnight, which stormed.
They are very handsome in their buckskin robes.
They sat and smoked by the fire and told their tales.

They were puzzled by our goose that sleeps inside.
I told them about the wolf. They said it was an omen.
A black wolf is a sign of good hunting in the winter
In the morning we ground beans and drank coffee.

They have certainly changed the pace of our day.
They've been good friends since we've been here.
I feel at ease when their winter camps are close.
It is time for me to return to my work or be late.

Tell the children we are grateful for their letters.
I will send them another silly rhyme with this letter.
Andrew sends a letter to Jacob and Rachael and you.
I love you all dearly and give Beth my gratitude.

The Wolf

I'm sorry to hear that Beth is ill. Give her my love.
This winter has been bitter cold these last months,
Andrew loves his letters from Rachael and Jacob.
It appears they both should become aspiring artists.

I've been able to work more on my new assignment.
Andrew's help has given me time to work at my desk.
I lose some time dreaming of my family so far away.
With every word,, I hold you close to my heart.

Today I awoke to the screeching of the birds.
I ran to the door. The black wolf stood by the cabin.
At first, he didn't move when I opened the door.
Then he walked away, looking back at me all the time.

Then, not so far away, he stopped and turned around.
I stepped out with my musket; Andrew at my side.
But he was not afraid and the birds became silent.
I set my musket aside and he lay down in the snow.

Since then, Andrew has given our scraps to the wolf.
He walks toward the hill and the wolf comes to him.
He runs in circles; then crawls forward on his belly.
I hope the spring thaw won't see his wolf go away.

I haven't seen the little minks that raid our eggs,
and there's been no wolverine tracks in over a year.
The Ojibwe must be right about the wolf's omen.
I've included these events in my articles.

The Juno sails April 25 for Montreal. I cannot wait.
I pray you have good sailing when this spring arrives.
I will meet you in Le Sault with the wagon and Jolie.
I send my love, and Andrew sends his letters, too.

(The Journey)

Leaving for Le Sault

It is almost June as I prepare to leave to Le Sault.
I have loaded my bags on the carriage wagon.
Our work horse, Jolie, will get us there and back.
Andrew has his horse and he'll be safe for a week.

As I ride away, Maggie flies after me and then stops.
She's a beautiful bird but too attached to us humans.
It will take me almost three days to get to Le Sault.
I've brought some firewood for evening camp.

I have taken the Indian trail through the woodlands.
The forest is dense: the sun barely shines through.
On the first night, I've found a good place to sleep.
I pull my wool and buckskin blankets over my face.

The early morning chill inspires me to make coffee.
Sitting by my campfire, I can hear the forest awake.
Writing in this journal is secondary to my thoughts.
My mind dwells on and imagines our coming reunion.

It is midday and I've pulled the wagon off the trail.
We both need a rest, and there is fresh water here.
As I begin to build a fire, I hear sounds in the trees.
Through the forest and brush I see runners on foot.

I can see they're a small party of Iroquois warriors.
They are intruders in this territory of the Ojibwa.
I keep Jolie quiet as they move away to the north.
I count my blessings that they have not seen me.

The Fur Trader

I have moved quickly south on the old wooded trail.
I watch constantly for more Iroquois till nightfall.
Finally I have found the trade route to Le Sault.
I make camp in the trees near the great lake's shore.

I awaken early to the light and sounds of daybreak.
There is traffic on the route near my campsite.
I have made a small fire to ward off the early chill.
Jolie is thirsty and I take her to the shore to drink.

A trader rides along the road and bids me good day.
He is a half-breed bedecked in a costume of furs.
He is a foreboding man, but I find humor in his garb.
I invite him to my camp and we have coffee and talk.

His name is Edmond. He travels from Thunder Bay.
He talks about his trappings on the way to Le Sault.
I tell him about my journey and the Iroquois party.
"They'll take your scalp for sport," he warns me.

After coffee, he leads his horse back to the road.
As he walks away in his furs he looks to be a bear.
Jolie is ready to go as I harness her to the carriage.
The new road is smooth and we are making good time.

I can hear the rapids of the Marie in the distance.
Hunger entices me to travel down into the village,
but it is late and I decide to make one last camp.
Under my blankets, I listen to the sound of rapids.

179

Le Sault

The morning sun warms my face and awakens me.
Below, I see the village of buildings and wigwams
laid out along the waters edge by the river Marie.
Across the river I see the big American buildings.

Jolie is as anxious as I, it seems, to end this trip.
Riding down the road to the crossing at the river,
I sing sweetly to her as she prances happily along.
To the southwest I see the white- capped rapids.

I've found livery for Jolie and a tavern by the inn.
Near the river crossing there is a border station.
The gentleman there knows of all incoming traffic.
Like an old town crier he informs the village of news.

I've put up at the inn and paid for my first bath.
The river seems empty without canoes or barges.
The noise and the smell of the tavern attract me.
Thinking of Lorraine makes me seek out company.

The tavern is the man's social ground in any town.
A table in the corner, with my journal, is all I need.
I can smell the scent of Edmond from yesterday,
And, indeed, I see him drinking across the room.

It's a tavern of traders, dock men and travelers.
Pints and food are being served by young women.
Edmond, only partly sober, wanders to my corner.
Tonight, I will drink. There'll be no more writing.

The Juno

It's the next morning as I sleep in my drunken dreams.
The rapping, rapping at the door of my room wakes me.
"Monsieur Brousard! There's news of a tragedy at sea"
I leap from the bed to the door. "What is it? When? "

The clerk, red faced, stares at my lack of clothes.
"A lost ship, sir. Off the coast. Last week's storm."
I throw on my clothes and run out to find a crowd.
"Does anyone know the name of the ship?" I ask.

An old hand, who looks to be a dockman, answers.
"It were called the Juno. That's word from Montreal".
My heart is about to burst. "Are there survivors, sir?"
"They've found none. Just floating bits and pieces."

Walking away from the crowd, my thoughts collide
between disbelief and exploding grief and deep anger.
I must wait for further news or my mind will not rest.
At the Tavern I find Edmond again. And again, I drink.

There is much talk about the Juno, but nothing new.
As the day drags on, I find myself falling into stupor.
The sounds of the tavern are deafening and confused.
Finally, I find myself being carried out and away.

I think it is Edmond who has brought me to my room.
On the bed, I watch the ceiling spinning above me.
The hard liquor has left me unable to move or think.
It is growing dark and I have lost sight of the room.

The Last Day

    I am waking out of my sleep in the sweat of my bed.
    The afternoon sun beats in through the windows.
    In the chair, across the room, Edmond is snoring.
    My head throbs and I sink my face in the wash basin

            "Wake up, Edmond. We've slept through the day."
              Even after he has sold and rid himself of all his pelts.
              Edmond still smells like the carcasses of dead animals,
       "I've sent for the innkeeper to bring you a bath."

    The tavern voices are loud with yesterday's news
    It's no good to listen to all this. The tragedy is done.
    That was the moment I admitted they were gone.
    I say adieu to Edmond and go to see how Jolie's doing.

Jolie dances when she sees me walk up to the livery.
Her stall is large enough for three. She is content.
She takes an apple from my hand and eats it down.
Knowing I've hidden another, she nuzzles my pockets.

I tell her we will leave tomorrow, early in the morning.
Talking to my horse has always helped clear my mind.
It is hard to explain, but the horse knows what I say.
But this time, I've bared all my soul and grief to her.

The air is warm and wet as I walk back to the inn.
Tears are flowing down my face as I think of them.
There is a picture in my mind that will never vanish.
I'll take my sorrow when I leave this place tomorrow.

185

Going Home

Morning is cool as I leave Le Sault in the early hours.

There is no news from the gentleman at the station.

"We will send you any word." he says, as I ride away.

Looking back I am saying, "Adieu, my sweet Lorraine"

      I have taken the old route home along the great lake.

      I stop in a place where the water meets the road.

      Jolie drinks her share and I fill my satchels with water.

      Two trappers tell me of a trail to take to the northeast.

I have a day and a half left of travel back to my home.

This new trail is wide and easy for us both to travel.

It is midday when I stop to rest my horse and myself.

As I rest, I try to write to clear my mind of misery.

      No matter how hard I try, the words will not come out.

      There is too much inside that keeps my pen from writing

      Instead, I gather needed kindling for the evening camp.

      My Jolie waits and chomps greedily on the greenery.

I have been traveling for hours through the woodlands.

At last, I've come upon a trail crossing east and west.

I've made a clearing for my camp beside the trails.

In a mindless daze I sit beside my fire and try to write.

I wonder how I will tell Andrew what has befallen us.
I wonder to myself how I will go on living without them.
Except for the boy, there appears no reason to stay on.
Our Ojibwa neighbors and friends will be very sad.

The Dream

It is growing dark and I see a hunting party coming.
I recognize the young one as Okemos, "Little Chief."
Another I know as Mingan, "Grey Wolf." Good boys,
no older than Andrew or Jacob, but already men.

Jacob had often gone night fishing with these two.
Tonight, I will have to tell them what has happened.
I welcome them to my camp and we sit about the fire.
Okemos and Mingan are deeply saddened and silent.

Night falls and I am sleeping in the carriage wagon.
The Indians have fallen asleep around the campfire.
I am thinking of my family when I fall into a dream.
In the dream I am at sea in the middle of a great storm.

I see a steamer in the midst of giant rolling waves.
There are lifeboats breaking away from the decks.
People are being swept off and into the angry ocean.
Alone on deck, I see Lorraine, Rachel and Jacob.

A single wave, higher than the ship, smashes over it.
When it is gone there is nothing left to see but ruin.
I scream out loud in my sleep and bolt up straight.
By the fire, the Indians leap to their feet in alarm.

I apologize and tell them of the nightmare I have had.
Mingan says we must sit by the fire again and smoke.
The ritual and the tobacco help to calm my spirit.
Okemos says, "They will be alive in your visions."

At the Ojibwe Camp

The Indians are up and awake too early for my habits.
"There'll be no coffee for us this morning," I tell Jolie.
We make a sight with dogs running beside the carriage
loaded with sleds, furs, Indians and a French driver.

> This woodland trail has little room for the carriage.
> The forest is dense and the sun barely shines through.
> It's rays flickering through the leaves on and off.
> It is late afternoon when we reach their summer camp.

I am relieved to see they are camped on a small lake.
There are seven birchbark wigwams made with saplings.
Canoes lay about and naked children play by the shore.
Men are roasting fish. Women are busy tanning skins.

    Little Chief takes me away to meet a very old man.
    Much of the Anishinabe language is unknown to me,
    When I am introduced to 'Nixkamich', I am puzzled.
    Okemos smiles at me, "It means Grandfather"

Nixkamich invites us all to sit inside around his fire.
Other men join us and the pipe is passed in a circle.
I feel I am being honored as I sit beside Nixkamich.
Both Okemos and Mingan sit proudly at his right side.

.

I try to understand the words as the old man speaks.
He tells of the first fathers' journey across the earth
and how they were chased by a giant fish to this land.
"It was when the water was as hard as stone." He says.

Food and tales

An old woman opens the door-flap and orders us to eat.
We have a meal of wild rice, roasted fish and berries,
Mostly everyone squats around the open fire pit to eat.
I thank them all for their good foods and hospitality.

Some, but mostly the children, are attracted to Jolie.
She becomes the evening sport for children to ride.
Jolie is uneasy and I have to keep her in check.
I let her drink and groom her. Soon the play is over.

A full moon plays brightly in the sky as I retire at last.
The Indians will stay awake for hours, but I must rest.
I write about this day and the warmth I've felt here.
I'm not ready to write about the sorrow I feel inside.

The night comes late with a chilling light breeze.
I lie back and look up at an incredible full moon.
Pulling up the blankets, I am in my own nest.
I hear muffled chatter and Jolie's snorting sounds.

I am almost afraid to go to sleep and have that dream.
Waking the whole village would not be a grateful thing.
But I am tired and this day has been longer than most.
After some time, sleep comes and I fall into a dream.

>In this dream, I am in a great canoe with the Ojibwa.
>Oil burns in a large clay pot in the middle of the canoe.
>We row past a wall of ice; one stands armed at the bow.
>A great whale with fire on his breath follows behind us.

Taking the River Trail

The warmth of the sun makes me sweat in my blankets.
Sounds of children; the scent of fish and water wake me.
I pull myself up to see several children standing by Jolie.
They all jump and laugh when they see my morning face.

I have cleaned up and I've gone to thank Nixkamich.
He is pleased to hear I saw his ancestors in my dream.
Okemos and Mingan ask to travel with me to my cabin.
By the time we reach there, it will be almost evening.

We take a trail away from the lake along the river bank.
At first the boys are running and racing beside me.
But the sun has grown warm and now they ride with me.
We are close to home when we stop for Jolie to drink.

Through the woods, Mingan sees movement in the trees.
We each worry that there may be Iroquois in the woods.
Okemos and Mingan ready their bows as we crouch low.
I have my flintlock loaded and squat under the carriage.

But Jolie walks off with the wagon and I am in the open.
Like Okemos and Mingan, I find shelter behind a tree.
Then, walking toward us, I recognize a familiar figure.
"Jean Pierre!" Andrew shouts. "Is that you Jean Pierre?"

We all ride in the carriage down the trail to the cabin.
Andrew sits beside me and I tell him about the family.
He tries to hold back, but tears flow down his face.
As we ride home, Andrew is silent and shakes his head.

The Cabin

Waiting for us at the cabin, there is a familiar sight.
Maggie stands tall and flutters her wings in greeting.
The other birds gather near the hillside and screech.
Higher up I see the black wolf standing by the old tree.

    It has grown dark and Andrew makes a fire in the stove.
    We have fish, and vegetables from Lorraine's garden.
    I am not sure of the wisdom in letting the Indians drink,
    But, after we eat, we share a bottle of wine together.

Okemos and Mingan laugh and wrestle on the floor,
but they calm down as the effect of the wine wears off,
Andrew is more amused by this than I, but I laugh, too.
I cannot think in all this journey when I last laughed.

    Andrew takes the scraps outside to feed to his wolf.
    It's a sweet sight to see the bond between the two.
    Okemos shouts out to Andrew from the cabin porch.
    "You are Black Wolf now, like Mingan is Grey Wolf."

It is Mingan's idea that they should go night fishing.
I stay at home but give them the lantern to lure the fish.
They'll go to the pond and stand on the rocks with spears.
The fish will swim to the light and they'll have a catch.

    I remember a time I went with Jacob and these two.
    They hung there leggings and loincloths on a tree.
    Jacob walked around the edge and softly beat the water.
    Mingan held the lantern. Okemos held the spear.

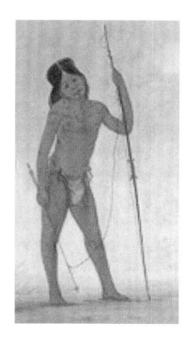

Pictures of my family

Alone, I hold the picture of my family in my hands.
The sadness I have hidden bursts forth in tears.
I sit at my desk and watch as my hands tremble.
I feel there is nothing I can write with these hands

It is late and the boys are still fishing at the pond.
I remember when Lorraine and I were first in love.
We had gone hopping down the rocks to the pond.
In the afternoon sun we had made love by the shore.

It was our first year at the cabin when the Ojibwa came.
It was Namida (Star Dancer) who brought the babies.
"You have children now," he said. "You have made none."
"They are not ours. They are Ottawa with no mothers."

They called them Onaiwah (Dove) and Achak (Spirit).
I think we were both in love with them at first sight.
We gave them French names and raised them as our own.
Our deep bond with the Ojibwa began that very moment.

Mingan and Okemos were the same age as our children.
It was natural that they should grow up together.
But, if they were not to be Ojibwa, they were to be us.
It has been two years since they left to learn in Paris.

I can no longer sit here and reflect on the past.
I change the straw in Maggie's box and she climbs in.
Sprawled across my bed I try to picture my family.
I see many images of a better time as I fall asleep.

Morning

Andrew brewing coffee on the stove awakens me.
Mingan and Okemos are petting Maggie's feathers.
More than coffee, the cabin smells of gutted fish.
"You have much to eat, Jean Pierre," Okemos smiles.

Outside washing my face in the basin, I see the wolf.
He is on the hill pouncing on the ground with his paws.
This is how I've seen him drive a mole from its tunnel.
Hunting rodents and Andrew's scraps keep him alive.

The aroma of fresh coffee draws me back inside.
The boys are sitting around the stove looking tired.
I sit with them cross-legged and we drink our coffee.
Mingan takes out his calumet and fills it with tobacco.

The coffee and the tobacco make my head is spin,
but, the pipe is passed around until it is emptied.
They stand up and Okemos says, "We will go now,"
"Someday, soon, you and Black Wolf will visit us."

Andrew smiles broadly when he hears his new name.
Standing at the cabin door we watch them walk away.
At first, they walk slowly, and then they decide to race.
We watch them run until they disappear into the woods.

Andrews Family

Andrew with his hand on my shoulder looks serious.
"I have something to tell you, Jean Pierre," he says.
"While you were gone my father came to take me back."
"And what did you tell him, Andrew? Will you go?"

Andrew did not look puzzled nor did he shake his head.
Andrew's father had found settlement to the north.
He came to the cabin only days before I arrived.
His mother and sisters were already making a home.

"I told him I would come after you had returned."
My heart sank some at the prospect of Andrew gone.
"But that was before all of this happened, Jean Pierre."
"What will you do now, Andrew? Will you go there?"

Maggie stood on the porch beside us as we talked.
I picked her up and held her for a moment and let her go.
We both smiled when she handed clumsily like a goose.
"If you allow it, Jean Pierre, I will stay here with you."

For me, this was not an easy request to answer.

Andrew's and my family had been friends for years.

"I don't want to cause a rift with your father," I said.

"When he hears of your tragedy, he will understand."

These words lifted my spirits and gave me warmth.

"I want you to stay, Andrew. You are a good friend."

"And tell me, son. How would I survive here alone?"

"You would write, Jean Pierre. And you would survive"

The summer days were hot this year and write I did.

Andrew and Maggie and his wolf made good company.

My thoughts of my family never fades from my mind.

And so I wrote these words:

In my nights

And in the visions of my dreams

they all live again within me,

just as Okemos wisely said.

In these visions I see them.

and for those few moments

I can hold them close

and we are together.

These dreams give me solace

and hope in my heart.

It's a place where we can meet

until I awake and they are gone.

I will dream of them again

and again, until I dream no more.

When that day finally comes
we will all be together forever.
August 30, 1840

Ojibwa cave painting circa 6000 B.C.

The End

A few reviews posted in Amazon/books of earlier books by Je. Corseau

Resurrecting the Muse

An excelent addition to any poetry collection! T. Coolidge

One of the best books of poetry i have read. Highly recommend this work' One should also read "Articles Pour Le Poste" I. Guyer

Thought provoking and enjoyable read. J Humphreys

I highly appreciated reading this piece of literature. Throughout it, the life journey of the author is revealed with each poem. Also, reading through the introduction was quite helpful to the reading of the entire book. This was a truly moving book. j. Guyer

An excelent addition to any poetry collection!

I haven't finished Resurrecting The Muse yet, and already its ranking among my favorites!
Its a great addition to any collection.
No self respecting poetry lover should pass this one up! P. Mandell

Happy, Sad, Funny, Interesting....

I highly recommend reading Resurrecting The Muse. It will entertain you, make you want to cry, make you want to laugh and is always, above all, interesting. I thoroughly enjoyed the ride...M Corsaut

...... this was a JOY to read. Beautiful, unique, thoughtful, and even a little funny. I highly recommend it! S Zehr

Resurrecting the muse is an incredible book of poetry. I savored every word and phrase. I highly recommend. Z Gibson

Letters To Lorrain/ Kindle Edition

Interesting historical work -translated from French with an Ojibwa theme. N.Ormateur

Article Pour Le Poste

As an artist I find Corseau"s work very moving, I am inspired by it and can not put it down, I am currently on Letter to Lorrain, very moving. P. Bongiorno

J. Corseau has an amazing soul with an addictive personality. i am blessed to have read this man, and will forever save a spot in my heart with his memories… W.Stone

Write your own review

If you want to help promote this book and the poetry of Je Corseau, go to www.amazon.com and type in Je Corseau

There you will be able to write a review of this anthology.

It would be greatly appreciated.

Intro to Resurrecting the Muse 2008

Introduction

The forms and styles of poems and vignettes here are sometimes so conflicting that I don't know how I thought I could incorporate them in a single edition. I simply felt there was a common thread throughout all of them.

I enjoy the fact that in poetry I can have the license to cheat the rules of language. That allows for the freedom to use any style that fits the nature of the poem. There are times when I wonder if poetry has any rules at all.

Like all arts, poetry evokes images and feelings and memories in its melodies of rhyme and prose. There is always a rhythm and flow to go with the words to create a mind's imag. Perhaps that's the rule.

There had also been a large volume of poetry written in Berkeley and North Beach in the 1960s. There had been many readings in coffee houses and book stores and on the streets of The Haight and Telegraph Avenue. Those were presented to a mixed bag of students, hippies and beatniks. In the cafes, always small and dim, with a small riser for performers, reading poetry, with the aid a guitarist or a flutist playing alongside, there were always good donations to be made and shared. And sometimes it was standing on the street with a basket and my manuscript.

Finally I had traveled south to Los Angeles in 1969 with the idea of recording an album of poetry . I took a small tape recorder with a taped demo of two poems recorded in Berkeley and proceeded to play it for anyone who would listen.

A friend I had known while attending Pasadena Playhouse had already developed a career in music. He introduced me to the people in the record business I would later work with. My record career was brief. The Age of Astrology was the first album, and it was released in England but not in America. The second album was produced at Harmony Recorders, but, because of disagreements, the production was cancelled and all the sessions handed to me. I still have those old masters and doubt they could be revived.

Now that this introduction has gone beyond academic value and become the beginning of a tale, I might as well mention that most of that original manuscript was lost in 1973. It came up missing while leaving Los Angeles somewhere between West Hollywood and Buelton on Hwy 101. Much of the selected poetry found in the first part of this book had already been separated from the main manuscript and was saved.

Je. Corseau

books of poetry by Je Corseau

"Resurrecting The Muse"2008
"Articles Pour Le Poste" 2010
"The Last Great Poet Laureate of the Mythical
                    State of Jefferson USA" 2019
Je Corseau Complete (anthology) 2024

https://www.amazon.com